Catiline

ANCIENTS IN ACTION

Boudicca
Marguerite Johnson

Catullus
Amanda Hurley

Cleopatra
Susan Walker and Sally-Ann Ashton

Hadrian
James Morwood

Hannibal
Robert Garland

Horace
Philip D. Hills

Lucretius
John Godwin

Martial
Peter Howell

Ovid: Love Songs
Genevieve Lively

Ovid: Myth and Metamorphosis
Sarah Annes Brown

Pindar
Anne Pippin Burnett

Sappho
Marguerite Johnson

Spartacus
Theresa Urbainszyk

Tacitus
Rhiannon Ash

Catiline

Barbara Levick

BLOOMSBURY
LONDON • NEW DELHI • NEW YORK • SYDNEY

Bloomsbury Academic
An imprint of Bloomsbury Publishing Plc

50 Bedford Square	1385 Broadway
London	New York
WC1B 3DP	NY 10018
UK	USA

www.bloomsbury.com

BLOOMSBURY and the Diana logo are trademarks of Bloomsbury Publishing Plc

First published 2015

© Barbara Levick, 2015

Barbara Levick has asserted her right under the Copyright, Designs and Patents Act, 1988, to be identified as Author of this work.

All rights reserved. No part of this publication may be reproduced or transmitted in any form or by any means, electronic or mechanical, including photocopying, recording, or any information storage or retrieval system, without prior permission in writing from the publishers.

No responsibility for loss caused to any individual or organization acting on or refraining from action as a result of the material in this publication can be accepted by Bloomsbury or the author.

British Library Cataloguing-in-Publication Data
A catalogue record for this book is available from the British Library.

ISBN: PB: 978-1-47253-489-7
ePDF: 978-1-47252-777-6
ePub: 978-1-47253-106-3

Library of Congress Cataloging-in-Publication Data
A catalog record for this book is available from the Library of Congress.

Typeset by Fakenham Prepress Solutions, Fakenham, Norfolk NR21 8NN

To Ray and Judy Forsyth
in whose garden I began to write this book

Contents

Chronology	viii
Preface	xi

1	Prologue: An Italian City under Roman Siege	1
2	Rome after Sulla	9
3	Politicians and their Problems	19
4	Catiline's 'First Conspiracy', 66–64	35
5	The Catilinarian Conspiracy of 63	41
6	The Aftermath of Catiline: Cicero's Struggle to Survive	87
7	Historiography and Villainy	109

Further Reading	125
Index	131

Chronology
(all dates BC)

146	Destruction of Carthage by P. Scipio Aemilianus.
133	Tribunate and murder of Tiberius Gracchus.
123–21	Tribunates and murder of Gaius Gracchus.
?108 (or 106)	Birth of Catiline.
106	Births of Cicero and Pompey the Great.
100	Sixth consulship of C. Marius. Lynching of L. Appuleius Saturninus and C. Servilius Glaucia. Birth of C. Julius Caesar.
91	Tribunate and assassination of M. Livius Drusus. Outbreak of Social War.
89	Siege of Asculum.
88	First consulship (joint chief magistracy) of L. Cornelius Sulla. Outbreak of Civil War.
86	Seventh consulship and death of Marius.
83	Sulla's return from the east.
82–81	Defeat of Marians; Sulla becomes Dictator and establishes Senate in power.
80	Sulla's second consulship and his retirement.
?80	Pompey's first military Triumph.
?78	Catiline holds quaestorship (junior magistracy, qualifying for membership of Senate).
78–77	Consulship and rebellion of M. Aemilius Lepidus.
77–71	Pompey in Spain defeating rebel forces under Q. Sertorius.
74–71	Revolt of slave gladiator Spartacus.
70	M. Licinius Crassus and Pompey, consuls, restore power of tribunes (representatives of the plebs).

68	Catiline praetor (second highest magistracy, carrying *imperium*, power of command).
67	Catiline governor of province of Africa. Lex Gabinia gives Pompey command against the pirates.
66	Cicero praetor (magistrate with power second only to that of consuls). Lex Manilia gives Pompey command against Mithridates VI Eupator of Pontus.
66–65	'First Catilinarian conspiracy'.
65	Catiline acquitted of misgovernment in Africa.
66–63	Pompey defeats Mithridates.
64	Catiline fails to be elected consul. Catiline acquitted on murder charge.
63	Cicero consul. Catiline's second failure to be elected consul (July). Conspiracy predicted and revolt of Manlius (21 and 27 October); *SCU* Meeting at Laeca's house (6 November) and alleged assassination attempt to follow. *In Cat.* 1, to Senate (8 November); Catiline leaves Rome. *In Cat.* 2, to People (9 November). Catiline reaches Manlius and is declared public enemy (mid-November). Defence of Murena. Allobroges arrested on bridge (3 December). *In Cat.* 3 to People; 4 to Sen. (3–5 December): interrogation, executions, rewards to witnesses.
62	Defeat and deaths of Catiline and Manlius. Pompey returns from the east.
61	Trial of P. Clodius Pulcher for infringement of Bona Dea rites.

59	Julius Caesar's first consulship. Recognition of 'First Triumvirate' of Caesar, Pompey and Crassus.
56	Renewal of 'First Triumvirate'.
55	Second consulships of Crassus and Pompey.
49	Outbreak of Civil War.
48	Pompey, defeated by Caesar, is assassinated in Egypt.
48–44	Caesar Dictator; assassination on 15 March 44.
43	Formation of 'Second' Triumvirate of Mark Antony, M. Lepidus and Octavian.
37	Renewal of Triumvirate.
31	Octavian defeats Antony and Cleopatra VII of Egypt at Actium.
30	Deaths of Antony and Cleopatra in Alexandria.
29	Triple Triumph of Octavian.
27	Restoration of a functioning constitution completed. Octavian takes name of 'Augustus'. Beginning of the 'Principate' – the Roman Empire of the first three centuries AD.

Preface

Lucius Sergius Catilina is the equivalent of Britain's Guy Fawkes. Both villains planned the overthrow of governments (63 BC and AD 1605). Both failed, died along with fellow-conspirators, and became bogeymen whose names resounded down the centuries in their own societies and beyond. The atrocity of the offences and the danger they presented made them unforgettable.

The parallel with Guy Fawkes is not exact: Catiline was more than the foot-soldier Fawkes, and whatever he planned (slaughtering the magistrates, burning the city, seizing power) lacked the overtly religious dimension of the English conspiracy; but it adds to the reasons for examining the affair, which are already powerful. First, the conspiracy of 63 led to the formation of the 'First Triumvirate' of 59, the informal and destructive alliance between Marcus Licinius Crassus, Gnaeus Pompeius (Pompey the Great) and Gaius Julius Caesar; so it was a significant event in the fall of the Roman Republic and the establishment of the Principate under Augustus, a monarchical form of government that was to mutate and survive in the eastern half of the Roman Empire until the fall of Constantinople to the Turks in 1453. Second, it was the subject of work by two literary giants, Cicero (106–43 BC), whose oratory was crucial in bringing about the execution of the senatorial conspirators, and Sallust (c. 86–35 BC), the historian who devoted his first great monograph to it. Third, it offers some of the pleasures of a detective story, with divergent and gappy evidence written up of course by the winning side and providing a teasing problem of 'unreliable narrators'. The received version, Cicero's, was followed uncritically until the later nineteenth century, when E. A. Beesly, a radical Professor at London University, reversed the roles of hero and villain and turned Catiline into a popular champion. Controversy flamed on. Like Guy Fawkes, Catiline and his followers have champions who argue for a frame-up. Two alternative versions of this view have proved persuasive: K. Waters', that the consul Cicero invented the threat to the Republic in order to qualify for a position equal or superior to those of its two leading politicians, Pompey the Great and M. Licinius Crassus; R. Seager's that he provoked an insurrection in order to deal with it, bringing dissidents into the open before Pompey returned with an army from the east. Yet Cicero's version, embodied in the literature, still attracts defenders. Posing the dilemma itself risks falling into the 'fallacy of false dichotomous questions' damned by D. H. Fischer. We have some incontrovertible facts buried in a mass of allegations about what was going on; with varying interpretations of what the actors intended. Controversies of the time have been reported by historians parroting received opinions and vulnerable to this day to their own political prejudices.

Beyond specific problems we find a large-scale tragedy, directly involving the entire political class and eventually bringing it down to humiliation and near-impotence. The individual villain of this episode is part of something grander, the playing out of a drama of ambition and envy that goes back to the legend of Romulus: who killed his twin Remus, co-founder of the city, for jumping over Romulus' walls. Every Roman in a sense was a man of action: he stood in the voting assembly – and at a signal could pick up his shield and become a fighting soldier. Catiline was not the only man of action in this story: Pompey, who enjoyed three Triumphs, was a supreme man of action – less good with words; while Cicero the orator performed one action during his consulship of 63 that was to have powerful consequences and perhaps gave him strength at the end of his life 20 years later to resist the approach of autocracy in the form of Mark Antony and the future Augustus.

MARIUS AND THE CICEROS

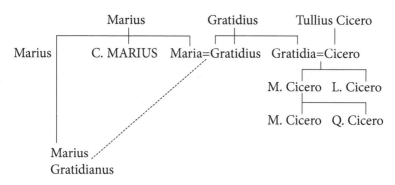

In denying the Catilinarian conspiracy a religious dimension I am far from denying the importance of religion in Roman life. Rome's link with her gods and the role played by women as well as men in maintaining them, and so assuring the survival and success of the community, guaranteed both the community itself and the individuals who held the key positions of responsibility and power that we meet again and again playing their leading roles in political life (as Vestal Virgins, Pontifices, Augurs, Flamines and the like, or guardians of boundaries between the sacred and the profane), which redoubled any merely secular influence that the upper class enjoyed.

We should be clear what we mean by 'conspiracy' and 'conspirator', dirty words that have elastic connotations when they are used by politicians, today as ever. In the *Oxford English Dictionary* a conspiracy is an agreement between two or more persons to do something criminal, illegal or reprehensible (especially in relation to treason, sedition or murder). The word 'reprehensible' itself has a certain elasticity. Far more slack comes in connexion with the participants and their roles, especially if the offended authority is actively vengeful and wide in its interpretations, as Cicero and fearful modern tyrannies are. A plan and action to carry it out should be required. Let us mentally preface the word 'conspirators' with 'alleged', until we see them in action.

xiv *Preface*

There is a chronology and guide to further reading. Technical terms are explained, and ancient place-names assigned their modern identifications. Political terms are more elastic. If I write of 'the Catilinarians', 'the Catilinarian conspiracy' and 'Catilinarian conspirators', when the problems are whether and when there was 'a' conspiracy at all, and how far it was 'Catilinarian', it is because we need categories, however provisional, to make it possible to refer to the individuals, alliances and events of the 60s BC.

Prologue: An Italian City under Roman Siege

Catiline and his comrades

In 89 BC three young men were serving as trainee officers in the Roman army that was besieging the north Italian town of Asculum (Ascoli Piceno) in the Marche. The war was a paradox. Italians were Rome's 'allies' (*socii*), who had contributed troops for their overseas wars – twice as many, they claimed, as the Romans themselves. But the Romans, government and individuals, had lorded it over the Italians. When public land was needed for distribution they took it back from allies long in possession, and defeated attempts to compensate them with grants of Roman citizenship. It was at Asculum in 91, after yet another such episode, that the allies' rebellion had begun: a visiting Roman magistrate was assassinated with his subordinate legate after threatening the people, and a Roman actor on stage had to joke his way out of the same fate. The 'Social' war was to cost, on one ancient estimate, more than 300,000 casualties, and it was to see the Romans yield to Italian demands for the citizenship.

The legions at the siege were commanded by a general who was a landowner native to the region. He was consul in 89 but hoped to prolong the power of this magistracy by taking control of a great war in the east against Mithridates VI of Pontus. Gnaeus Pompeius Strabo ('Squinter'), if he had not died as he hovered outside Rome, might have proved as brutal as his rivals for that command, Gaius Marius and Lucius Cornelius Sulla. But in mid-November Strabo granted Roman citizenship to a troop of Spanish cavalrymen, a reward for valour. The act required witnesses taken from his council and it was recorded on a bronze tablet, which survives. Two of them, key players in 63, were still messmates in a war that was both a symptom and a driving factor in the downfall of the Roman Republic.

Pompeius Strabo's son and apt pupil, Gnaeus Pompeius, 'Pompey', was designated Magnus, 'the Great' from the time he was sent to Spain in 77. Another attested witness was 'Lucius Sergius, son of Lucius, of the voting district Tromentina' – that is, Catiline, it is generally agreed. He may have been at least two years older than young Pompey: he reached the praetorship, one step below the consulship, in 68, and the minimum age for that was 40, unless, as a privileged patrician, he enjoyed a remission of two years. A third youth might have been present. In 89 he witnessed the unsuccessful negotiations between Strabo and a rebel commander, P. Vettius Scato, but he was transferred to Sulla's command in the south before the summer was out. This was Marcus Tullius Cicero, the budding orator and future statesman, Pompey's exact contemporary.

Marius and the Ciceros

When the three young men had eyed each other in the mess, there is no doubt who would have looked the least well off: Cicero, the *parvenu* from Arpinum, in spite of being a connexion of Marius. Starting as a member of the second order in the state, the *equites* ('knights'), well-off landowners and businessmen who did not normally aspire to membership of the Senate, he was destined for an arduous career through the senatorial magistracies; a gap of five years was left between 94 and the previous plebeian consul. Without military talent or ambitions, he would need money, honed oratorical

Prologue: An Italian City under Roman Siege   3

gifts for use in the law courts, and the repute and powerful friends to be gained by winning cases. As soon as Cicero had assumed a man's toga at the age of 16, his father sent him to Rome for training with one of the most eminent jurists of the day. He was in fine company, and in serving in Strabo's army he was showing patriotism. Whether he was curbing the wit that was to make him so many enemies is another matter.

If his ambitions had been military, Cicero would have been envious of his fellow officer Pompey. As the son of the consul Strabo, Pompey was supremely well placed to find positions on the staff of other Roman generals. But whether it was a lightning bolt or disease that carried Strabo off, his son was left with his father's wealth, his clients, and his troops. He also inherited his talent as a soldier, and the discipline to hone it. Plutarch paints him as a real professional, controlling diet, restricting visits to the baths, avoiding frivolous company: he would eat seated, not reclining on a couch like other Romans, and spent his nights studying strategy. Pompey inherited his father's enemies too, among the Marians, and during the interval between Sulla's departure for the war in the east and his vengeful return in 83 had to fight in the courts for his right to Strabo's inheritance. In any case Pompey had no taste for service under another general. When Sulla came back he offered his service with his own forces, three legions recruited from his native Picenum, and dependent on him for their livelihood after they were discharged. Using them he first operated with spectacular success in Italy and Africa and then claimed that it was their bullying that forced him to make demands on the central government: for himself a military Triumph. Bonds forged in Sulla's army, especially in Pompey's section of it, and in Pompey's forces in Spain in the seventies, may have developed into political alliances; useful officers were united by shared loyalty to their former commander. Aulus Gabinius (consul 58), who secured Pompey's command against the pirates in 67 and was with him in the east until 63, presents a career entwined with Pompey's; the Catilinarian conspirator Publius Gabinius Capito may have been a cousin.

Catiline's family

Of the three young men who served with Strabo in 89, Catiline was aware of being the best-bred – in his last months he made a scornful comparison of his own origins with those of Cicero. He belonged to a voting tribe associated with the city of Veii (Veio) in southern Etruria, but one that produced a number of patrician families; such families had originally dominated the Roman Senate. It was the equivalent of having ancestors who crossed the Channel with William the Conqueror. By the first century BC only about a third of the Senate were patrician, but even then some formal privileges remained: for example, a monopoly of certain priesthoods. There were disadvantages: no patrician could hold the tribunate of the plebs, an office devised to protect the lower orders from oppression and a very potent one in late Republican political struggles. Besides that, only one of the two annual consuls could be a patrician; one place was reserved for plebeians (such as Pompey and Cicero) since 342. For patricians no place was reserved.

In Virgil's *Aeneid*, Catiline's clan, the *gens Sergia*, is traced back to the Trojan Segestus, companion of Aeneas in his wanderings. Members had played a distinguished part in Roman military history, and Catiline is described by Sallust as 'noble': he was directly descended from a consul. But Marcus Sergius Silus, his great-grandfather, who was celebrated as the first person known to be equipped with a prosthetic hand, and had shone during the Second Punic War at the end of the third century, had reached only the praetorship. Another M. Silus, probably Catiline's grandfather, served

Prologue: An Italian City under Roman Siege 5

as legate to M. Aemilius Paulus in Greece (168). Catiline's father was impoverished and, unlike Pompey's, played no remarkable part in politics or war. There was an estate, or he would not have possessed the half-millon *sesterces* that were required even for members of the equestrian order, who ranked second in the state after the Senate. There must have been a number of slaves to work the estate and attend on him, besides other dependents, freedmen and other 'clients'. Certainly he seems to have married his older child into an equestrian family. Her blue blood enhanced the value of her dowry, vicious though one biased source makes Sergia. Like Julius Caesar (a descendant of Venus Genetrix), and indeed Sulla himself, Catiline belonged to a 'decayed' family, which had recently lacked the ability, friends or ready cash to advance members to the highest office. Even at the earliest stage of his career Catiline may have looked with envy at Pompey.

Personality

In the turbulent Late Republic, men burdened with ancestry were tempted to take risks. Character sketches, even casual references, make Catiline fit his time, but the most thorough were the work of Cicero during and after the crisis of 63 and of Sallust under Cicero's influence. Here is Cicero in 63, in his second speech against Catiline, presenting a smooth *bon viveur*:

> My last class [of Catilinarian conspirator] … is composed of men whose very type and way of life belong to Catiline. They are his recruits, or rather his cherished bosom friends. Their hair is well-combed; they are well-groomed; some are cleanshaven, others have a full beard; they wear tunics reaching their wrists and ankles; they drape themselves in veils, not togas. All they work at and concentrate on for their entire life and waking hours is banqueting till dawn. All

the gamblers and adulterers flock to them, the filthy and shameless. There lads have learnt not only how to make love – and have it made to them –, how to dance and sing, but how to brandish daggers and dispense poisons.

Seven years later, defending a young man charged with associating with Catiline, Cicero has a different perspective:

Many excellent young men followed that evil and unscrupulous person ... Caelius was an enthusiast for Catiline ... But many others, of all ranks and all ages, were the same. For that person, as I judge you remember, possessed a multitude of signs of exceptional qualities, not fully formed, but in outline. He made use of a number of men of no scruple, and yet pretended that he was devoted to the best. He presented a number of temptations to vice; but he did have certain means of stimulating concentration and hard work. Inside he was on fire with his lusts and the faults that went with them; but all the same he was keen to master the art of the soldier. I don't think either that there has ever been such a monster on this earth, compounded of such conflicting, divergent, and mutually inconsistent passions and desires. Who ever has been more agreeable to men of higher distinction, or more closely bound to lower? What citizen, once of the better cause, has proved a direr enemy to this state? Who has been more debased in his pleasures, more enduring in pursuing his aims? More miserly in his greed, more unstinting in his largesse? Those extraordinary qualities were present in that man ...: to embrace many as friends, attend to them loyally, share what he had with everybody, serve the needs of his people as they occurred with his money, influence, physical effort, even with criminal activity, if it were needed, or outrage; to adapt his own nature and turn it to the needs of the moment, to twist and turn one way or another, so as to live austerely with the serious-minded, obligingly with the tolerant, solemnly with his elders, merrily with the young, aggressively with the criminal minded, luxuriously with libertines ... He even almost deceived me – me! – for a while. He looked like a citizen of merit, one whose aims were of everything that was best, a firm and faithful friend.

Prologue: An Italian City under Roman Siege 7

Sallust's slant on Catiline also emphasized his power over the young, and the effect of guilt on his demeanour – Romans knew how criminals should look:

> He had incredible physical and mental strength, but in a wicked and depraved character ... His endurance was hardly to be believed: hunger, cold, sleep-deprivation; mentally he was bold, treacherous, and changeable; he could make a pretence of anything whatsoever or conceal it; he was greedy for others' property and squandered his own. His desires were flagrant. He could talk in public well enough, but lacked self-restraint. His wild temperament always made him long for the excessive, the incredible, and what was above his range ... He gave a thorough education in acts of wickedness to the young men he had caught; from them he provided false witnesses and forgers. They were to hold honour, property, and danger cheap; then, when he had eroded their good reputation and sense of decency, he exacted more and worse. If the motive for immediate crime was inadequate, he still entrapped and slaughtered innocent as well as guilty. Obviously he was evil and cruel without reason, rather than letting hands and minds lose their tone from idleness.

But it was his guilty conscience over a murder that branded him and, in Sallust's view, drove him on to his plot: 'Hence his bloodless complexion, ravaged eyes, and irregular gait. In a word, madness lurked in his face and expression.'

Here then was a suave, attractive, charismatic individual, versatile, intense, diligent, energetic, and courageous in the field. We should not make too much of the desperate physiognomy, though Catiline evidently had a strikingly intent expression. Noticeably, nothing is said of civil talents or intellectual interests. Even so, in the right circumstances birth and favour might have taken him to the heights of the consulship.

2

Rome after Sulla

Landownership and recruitment

The causes of the Social War were deep-rooted, and there were many problems it did not solve. From the mid-second century the issue of landownership and occupation was at the centre of Roman economic, social and political difficulties. As perceived by ancient historians, the small farmers who made up the strength of Rome's vital legionary forces were losing their land to big slave-run estates. Even without accepting that story as universally applicable, a second-century general did find it difficult to fill up his ranks, for distant and lengthy campaigning in Spain was not profitable. This was a problem that continued into the Principate (27 onwards) until the legions consisted largely of men enlisted from the provinces. Since 133 tracts of Roman public land, the Ager Publicus – taken from defeated enemies, but some of it land that Rome's Italian allies had long been allowed to treat as their own – had been claimed back from their occupiers. Populist politicians (dubbed *populares* and understood to be those who aimed at benefiting the people despite the Senate – whatever their motives) intended it to be divided among landless Romans, many of them discharged veterans, so ensuring long-term supplies of recruits. Both Tiberius Gracchus, tribune of the plebs in 133, and his younger brother Gaius and his associates in 123–21, who had offered the Italian allies Roman citizenship and its privileges in return for their public land, and initiated the famous grants of free grain to the people of Rome, had been murdered by their rivals, splitting the Roman people into two, Cicero thought. They had political successors. The latest to offer the Italians this deal, M. Livius Drusus, tribune in 91, was also assassinated, and the war with the allies broke out at the end of that year.

Scarcely any of the alleged causes of Rome's problems have been left unchallenged. In particular, depopulation, the shortage of men qualified by their property to join the legions, the extent of takeovers of small farms by large landowners using slave labour, made possible by new lengthy terms of service, even the exhaustion of the surplus of public land available for division, have justifiably been questioned. Field surveys have shown high-density rural settlement; estates using slaves needed free labour from their neighbours to supplement them. Nonetheless, although what happened may have been patchy and unrepresentative, symptomatic changes reported by Plutarch and Appian, whatever their causes, were perceived and resented, and caused alarm for the future of the Commonwealth. The Senate as a body was unable to deal with social and economic problems, not only because administrative machinery was insubstantial, but because it lacked the collective will to act. Legislation necessary for reform would have to be carried through public assemblies by individuals, who would take the credit and become unacceptably powerful: even their names would be immortalized in those of the laws they passed, as that of the Gracchi was in their Leges Semproniae.

Civil war at Rome

So the war of 91 led to new strife at Rome itself. Concessions of rights and privileges including full citizenship came in a series of laws (90–88) promoted by ambitious politicians; and the Roman voting system had to be modified to accommodate the new citizens – to the advantage of one politician or another. Enrolment was far from complete: no census was held until 70, nor again in the sixties and fifties.

Besides that there was the other struggle at Rome in the early eighties: a personal one, between generals who hoped to wage the war against Rome's aggressive rival for hegemony in Asia Minor: Mithridates VI. The consul of 88, L. Cornelius Sulla, killed his enemies and drove out his renowned but aging rival C. Marius. Marius' glory days had been at the end of the second century when he defeated threatening northern tribes, the Cimbri and Teutones; but he had distinguished himself again in the Social War. During Sulla's absence in the east, the surviving partisans of Marius, who had returned to Rome in vengeful mood but died early in his seventh consulship in 86, were dominant at Rome. In 83 Sulla brought his troops back from the east and crushed the Marians, following up his victory with a further series of systematic murders which eliminated his opponents, confiscated their property (the 'proscriptions' which, according to Julius Caesar, stuffed Sulla's followers full of wealth), and deprived their sons of political rights.

Sulla as Dictator in 81 restructured Rome's constitution, regulating the career of magistrates, the scope of pro-magistrates operating abroad, and especially making the tribunate of the plebs a powerless dead end. In another controversial change he removed the equestrian order from any share in the jury courts, which had been another source of conflict since the tribunate of Gaius Gracchus. As Sulla was said to have expressed it, 'I have put the Senate into the saddle; let us see if it can ride'. After inaugurating his restored constitution as one of the consuls of 80, he retired.

Party politics?

'Marians' is one of the loose terms that we need to identify Roman political groupings, which were fluid and propelled by the ambitions of individuals. There were no formal political parties, and men rallied to support kinsmen or individuals who they thought would look after their interests. Rivalries and opportunistic attacks were carried out of the Senate House into the Forum, the scene of informal speeches to the people, and to the law courts, where a young politician could make his name by felling an opponent on a charge such as electoral bribery, misgovernment of a province, or even the useful hold-all of bringing the state into disrepute – 'diminishing its majesty', presumably in relation to the 'majesty' of lesser states.

Young men of birth could reach the highest magistracy, the consulship, with the help of an unblemished record at home and abroad and a little largesse. They passed easily from the opening 20-man quaestorship, which after Sulla gave entry to the Senate and could be held at the age of 30, then perhaps through the aedileship (in charge of Rome's markets) or tribunate of the plebs, to the praetorship, which carried the power to issue compelling orders at Rome and to command in the field (*imperium*). That was available at the age of 40. Finally, at 42, two of the ex-praetors (raised by Sulla from six to eight) could hope for the consulship, whose superior *imperium* meant that holders were preceded by 12 attendants, the lictors, carrying symbolic bundles of rods, the *fasces* (praetors were attended only by six).

Competition was intense, much greater that it had been before Italian allies had been admitted to citizenship. Men frustrated at one election could increase their chances at the next by offering the people exceptional rewards, as the Gracchi did. Such bids, if made against the wishes of the Senate, made them almost demagogues, mistrusted *populares*. They might combine, or act in rivalry with each other. Senators who opposed their activities believed, rightly, that they were likely to destabilize the authority of the Senate, as envisaged in an idyllic past after the victory over Hannibal (202). Such conservatives termed themselves 'optimates' or '*boni*' (those who 'supported what was best' or were simply 'sound'). With their connotations of property and high morality, those were certainly not terms favoured by their opponents, for all Cicero's efforts to include meritorious but humble people in the optimates. '*Pauci potentes*', 'the few in power', was sufficient for Catiline in the harangue against the *boni* that Sallust puts into his mouth. Scholars used to impose a spurious binary structure on Roman politics by referring to 'optimates' and '*populares*', as if they were the equivalent of modern political parties. These informal terms were a shorthand to encompass politicians who at one time or another shared common aims. Views became polarized, and the terms served to distinguish two approaches to Rome's problems: one purporting to serve the interests of the People, the other championing rule by the Senate, supported by well-to-do conservatives in the equestrian order. (Cicero on the canvass spoke of his 'army' as consisting of the *boni* and well-off.) When Catiline was growing up the division was already clear. He began by showing himself a man of action who fought on the winning side, as a partisan of Sulla's optimate cause. By the end of his life he was labelled a desperate *popularis*, a man of action with a revolutionary purpose.

It can be imagined what the political, economic and social atmosphere of Rome was like in the years that followed Sulla's reforms, when his coterie was precariously supreme. Politicians were in exile, careers blighted, families ruined, even their rights as citizens as well as their property taken from them. Some Marians had fled to Spain and set up an alternative government under the leadership of Quintus Sertorius, an ex-praetor. The Sullan general Q. Metellus Pius was making only slow progress against them. There was even a suspicion that Sertorius might join forces with the resurgent Mithridates, whose successes in Asia were squeezing credit facilities and, along with the activities of pirates, damaging trade. Prices rose. In Italy there were areas attached to Marius that still regarded themselves as ill-used in the Sullan settlement: the penalty for resistance had been confiscation of the land in favour of Sulla's ex-soldiers. This created not only resentment among the dispossessed but also anxiety among the new possessors in case the law that conferred their right to land should be revoked; Faesulae (Fiesole) in Etruria was a focus of such resentments. Apart from these two groups, there was a class of landholders whose property had been confiscated but never actually divided up – those of Arretium (Arezzo) and Volaterrae (Volterra) were in this plight; when a tribune in 60 was putting forward an agrarian bill with a view to settling Pompey's eastern veterans, Cicero spoke for the exemption of these lands, while confirming the rights of Sullan colonists. His aim was not strict justice, but the decisive ending of disputes. Successful farming and investment in buildings and tools in existing conditions were not remotely likely.

The beneficiaries themselves were discontented. Some fell into debt, their dispossessed rivals claimed, because they were greedy, extravagant, and incompetent farmers. But their properties could not be mortgaged to raise money for implements and improvements. In 78 men from both camps were ready to follow the consul M. Aemilius Lepidus, who had fought under Sulla but was at odds with the oligarchy. He had already undergone a trial for misgovernment at which he was acquitted with the help of Pompey, who then helped him into a consulship. Pompey knew what he was doing. Sent to put down a rising in Etruria, Lepidus joined the rebels, who would have promised him another term in office if they were successful. They were not, and he died in Sardinia on his way to join Sertorius.

On the other hand, Sulla had confirmed the grants of citizenship to the Italians that had been made as a result of the Social War, and from his supporters and even from some Italians he had raised the number of the Senate to a notional 600. As he did not increase the number of higher magistracies proportionately, competition became even more bitter and bribery still more rife. Office became more expensive and aristocrats invested in land found themselves short of ready cash. They could not expect to gain more than 6 per cent a year from their estates, and inheritances were divided equally between the children of a paterfamilias. Young men needed money to launch their careers, and many were particularly badly off if their fathers were still alive and in total control of family fortunes – sons received only pocket money. If they borrowed, it would be at a high rate of interest (48 per cent is known). And now members of established families were faced by 'new men' who were always seen as rich – they needed to be. Some were newly enfranchised Italians, others Roman entrepreneurs who had done well in the wars. Charges of bribery, and laws against it, are prominent in the seventies and sixties. During the consular elections of 64 the Senate had proposed enhancing the penalty to deal with Catiline and his ally Antonius; that proposal had been vetoed by a tribune. The issue culminated in a bill brought in by Cicero in 63, the year of Catiline's last attempt on the consulship.

Shortage of cash, greed and competitiveness, salted with arrogance and sadism, made governors more likely than ever to mistreat their subjects. The case of C. Verres, prosecuted by Cicero in 70 for theft and violence in Sicily was a *cause célèbre*, and a black mark against the Sullan oligarchy. He was a gross offender, but it was normal for a politician to count on paying off his debts to money-lenders when he was sent to a province he could fleece.

The role of the people

So far we have considered individuals and privileged sections of society. What of the Roman People, to whom sovereignty was ascribed? Of Rome and Italy? In particular, what power did the Roman plebs of the city wield? That is a matter of debate, once regarded as settled: they were powerless in the grip of dominant families. Strong arguments have been brought forward to overthrow that view: Rome was essentially a democracy, with its two popular assemblies to elect magistrates and enact laws; politicians such as Cicero are attentive to the People's behaviour and hone their oratory to sway it.

The second-century Greek historian Polybius did not hold either view; he called the Roman Republic a 'mixed constitution', monarchical, aristocratic, democratic. There was also a difference between theory and practice. As to the people, a nuanced view should be taken. Of the two assemblies, one, the tribal assembly based on voting districts, was comparatively democratic – for voters who could reach Rome; the other, the 'centuriate', was divided into voting blocks based on property, the wealthiest voting first and having their choice made known to the rest; this was the body that voted for consuls and praetors. In the post-Sullan courts jurymen were picked by lot from members of the Senate. That was changed in 70, but the senators lost their monopoly to panels consisting of *equites* and other men of property. Again, pre-existing ties of clientship and deference counted; such vertical ties intersected the horizontal lines of class. And trade guilds and burial societies could work for patrons or hire themselves out to the highest bidder. On the other hand, strong surges of opinion (as on questions of land distribution or grants of citizenship, which affected the rights of 'ordinary' Romans) could call in masses from the fields to vote, upsetting previous conformations. Demonstrations broke out at the funeral of the *popularis* P. Clodius Pulcher in 52 and at Julius Caesar's in 44. Clodius, dubbed 'a Catiline with better luck', had been a master of the 'gangs' and it is hard to see where spontaneity ended and cash payments began. In the late sixties, the casual income of plebeians went down when Pompey secured his eastern command, making an end of his handouts, but lesser men paid what they could. Effectively popular election ended in AD 14, but the people were still a force to be reckoned with under the Empire, when they could make themselves felt in the theatre and at the games, as well as in the streets and round the Senate House.

Sallust paints a lurid picture of Catiline's desperate supporters. He can claim that despite two senatorial decrees and offers of rewards for information, nobody came forward and there were no desertions from Catiline's camp, an incredible claim after the execution of the five conspirators at Rome. The plebs were all in favour of Catiline, out of envy and because they had nothing to lose. But the city population was full of cheeky reprobates, spendthrifts, and those who had had to leave home for some criminal act. They had gravitated into a 'cess-pit', as the more fortunate called it. Some hoped to get the rewards of rank and wealth that Sulla's soldiers had received, and farm labourers left work to come to Rome and live on state and private doles. To these Sallust adds the men who had lost everything in the Sullan proscriptions. The tribunes, restored to power by Pompey and Crassus in 70, incited the plebs, and inflamed them more with their attacks on the Senate and their promises. Sallust's graphic account needs toning down, but there is truth in it and it reflects the picture entertained by the wealthy and respectable, who thought that they were under threat of imminent attack.

3

Politicians and their Problems

Cicero's progress

Cicero struck out from private cases in 80 by defending a man charged with parricide, Sextus Roscius of Ameria (Amelia). There was money in this case for Sulla's agents, who meant to get their hands on Roscius' inheritance. Cicero might well have been found dead in an alley, but he saved his client, launching the brilliant career as an advocate that brought him valuable connexions among A. W. Lintott's 'new rich' of the late Republic. Between 79 and 77 Cicero studied philosophy and oratory in Athens and Rhodes. In due course he entered the Senate as quaestor for 75 and then for 70 was elected aedile. That year he abandoned his previous role as a defence counsel and gave a cautious push to the reforming bandwagon by his devastating prosecution of the brutal governor of Sicily, C. Verres, who was defended by the leading optimate orator, Q. Hortensius. It was a test case, Cicero said, for senatorial juries and their last chance to show integrity. Verres threw up his defence and fled to Massilia (Marseille), and Cicero had made his name as a powerful political voice. Advancement for him, in a world in which the Sullan settlement was discredited and crumbling, lay with supporting popular causes, the commands of Pompey the Great against the pirates and Mithridates, his defence of Pompey's supporters at Rome.

Reaching the praetorship in 66, Cicero became intent on breaking down the barriers that kept a new man, especially one without military merit, from the consulship, for which his due year was 63. The 'new man' and friend of Pompey needed help from the most influential ranks of the aristocracy, the nobles whose vested interests in the traditional system made them natural optimates. These are the very men he describes in the second of his surviving letters to his close friend Titus Pomponius Atticus (?109–32), from mid-65, as being inimical to his candidature. And yet Cicero came top of the poll – all the voting centuries put him first – and became consul on 1 January 63. Something had come to his aid. His work for clients, some of them influential politicians, others rich equestrians, for the companies of tax-gatherers and contractors and the rest of the equestrian order from which he had sprung, benefited him. Other views lay stress on the undesirability of some of his competitors: the noble candidates were nonentities or disreputable, as were M. Antonius and Catiline himself, whom Cicero calls in an election speech 'two daggers plunged at the same time into the heart of the Republic'; and there were fears aroused in some senatorial quarters by the ambitions of M. Licinius Crassus and Julius Caesar, the future Triumvirs. Cicero at least had to offer a safe pair of hands.

Pompey and his father's example

Pompey's route to his consulship of 70 was very different. Sulla, even in his supremacy, when his constitution was scarcely minted, could not refuse a formal Triumph to a man still three or four years too young for the lowest magistracy: he had conquered Sicily and Africa for the optimate cause. Pompey had developed the technique he had learnt from his father, and practised in Africa: that of waiting until the prize he was after was put into his hands by a reluctant and

Politicians and their Problems

angry donor. After his first Triumph he had failed to disband his army until the Senate, desperate to rid Italy of M. Aemilius Lepidus, the ex-consul who had taken up the side of the Marians, asked him to join the generals in charge of that operation. Lepidus fled, but Sertorius' rebellion in Spain continued. Pompey had his supporters in the Senate. One of them was the senior consular (since 91) Q. Marcius Philippus, who was probably the speaker who urged that the general currently in charge of the campaign, Q. Metellus Pius, was 'too old'. (Pompey, of course, was 'too young'.)

After initial setbacks Pompey was completely successful, and his conciliatory attitude to the surviving rebels made him their potential champion with the oligarchy at Rome. On his return to Italy, by another stroke of luck, he was confronted by the famous slave revolt of the gladiator Spartacus, which M. Licinius Crassus was putting down after the failures of several other generals. Pompey gave the finishing touches to the campaign and the two men held Triumphs, Pompey's a full one, Crassus' in the minor form of an ovation, and both stood for the consulship of 70. Here at latest is the origin of the longstanding rivalry between the two Sullan generals.

Crassus had reached the required age of 42, Pompey was still only 36 and had never held another magistracy. Scholars, who justify the grant of such a concession to Pompey on the grounds of his past successes in the senatorial cause, fail to remember that those too had been possible only because Pompey had been in Italy with an army, and that Sulla's unqualified purpose had been to keep individuals with *imperium* in a regular succession of posts and to make them the obedient servants of a dominant Senate. The first consulship of Pompey and Crassus was distinctly radical and *popularis* in tone. They restored the plebeian tribunes to their full legislative powers, a colleague gave the equestrian order a share in the jury courts, and a tribune passed a bill restoring political rights to the followers of Lepidus. Not surprisingly, given the political rewards on offer from grateful beneficiaries, the consulship of Crassus and Pompey also became increasingly acrimonious in its courtship of the People and a meeting of *reconciliatio* had to be staged.

After his consulship Pompey did not take up a provincial command in the regular way but retired into private life, like General Charles de Gaulle at Colombey-les-Deux-Eglises; he wanted something better than a commonplace province and was waiting for his country to call him to her aid once again. The Mediterranean was swarming with pirates, who had taken advantage of Rome's preoccupation with the social and civil wars, kidnapping rich civilians from the Italian coast itself.

How could Pompey be called to his country's aid, when the Senate contained his bitter optimate enemies? Aulus Gabinius, one of the tribunes of 67 – whose power Pompey had helped to restore – put a law to the popular assembly nominating Pompey for the task, with equipment and subordinates. The work was achieved in 40 days, allegedly, and sealed with a merciful settlement of the survivors. But Pompey was not to return to Rome for five years. With the help of Cicero, another tribune, C. Manilius, in 66 passed a bill that enabled him to take on the more formidable Mithridates VI, resurgent in Asia Minor, invading the kingdom of Bithynia and giving one Roman general after another as much as they could cope with. Even with Pompey in charge of a war that his father had hankered to conduct, it was not until 63 that Mithridates was trapped and forced to suicide. At Rome, meanwhile, Pompey's tribunician agents were attacked in the courts – and defended by his old comrade in arms Cicero.

In the late 60s Pompey confronted serious problems. He knew he would have to be awarded another Triumph, but he wanted more that was in the Senate's gift. He must find land for the veterans he would be discharging in Italy: on that depended the credit he had with his men. Then there were the arrangements he had made in the east – most importantly his creation of new provinces, Pontus-Bithynia and Syria, and the city foundations that he had made there; on the periphery of the Empire were monarchies that depended on him for their legitimacy. These arrangements needed to be ratified by the Senate, which feared for its own supremacy. It contained enemies and rivals such as Crassus and L. Licinius Lucullus, whom Pompey had displaced as commander against Mithridates; there were the relatives of men for whose deaths 'the butcher boy' of the civil wars had been responsible. And Dio claims that Q. Metellus Celer, consul in 60, opposed the settlement, offended because Pompey had divorced his half-sister. At any rate there were enough men to put up a filibuster. On his side were the common people whom he had vindicated abroad and enriched with his contributions to a hard-pressed Treasury; and there would be more tribunes to put his case before them. How Pompey's settlement and his future career would shape was a question.

Catiline's sinister start: Murder and depravity

In the 80s Catiline gallantly followed Pompey's military example, but as a subordinate: he lacked Pompey's resources of men and money. He had been a tiro in Pompeius Strabo's army, turned away from the Marians, put his talent at the disposal of Sulla as a friend and zealous partisan, and served with distinction from 82 to 80. It was through Catiline that Sullan forces were successful in beginning the investment of an Italian city, either Praeneste (Palestrina) in 82 or further to the south Nola or Aeserina (Isernia). But what he did in the Sullan proscriptions was exceptionally hideous – if the stories circulated later are true. Catiline was in charge of a troop of Gauls exacting vengeance for Sulla. Amid a series of murders, including victims named by Cicero in his electoral speech and in a later pamphlet *On Electioneering*, at the end of the war in 82, that of M. Marius Gratidianus stands out. Tribune in 87 BC and twice praetor, Gratidianus had advocated economic reform, was nephew of Marius and allegedly the brother of Catiline's wife. He had prosecuted the leading optimate, L. Lutatius Catulus, a former colleague of Marius (consul in 100), when the Marians triumphed in 87 and Catulus suffocated himself rather than face conviction. Now Catiline cut off the head of Gratidianus, carried it through the city from the Janiculum to the temple of Apollo and delivered it to Sulla 'full of life and breath'. Later writers elaborate on the horrors: according to Plutarch, Catiline washed the blood off his hands at a nearby fountain sacred to Apollo. Plutarch also alleges Catiline's murder of a blood brother after Sulla's victory at the Colline Gate. Catiline persuaded Sulla retrospectively to add his name to the list of the proscribed – and in return killed Gratidianus. The 'brother's' death (otherwise unknown) is probably the creation of a careless copyist.

Certainly the deal with Sulla is unconvincing. Other accounts of Gratidianus' death, starting from Sallust's *Histories,* in which he is tortured and 'sacrificed' at Catulus' tomb, have no role for Catiline. It is only in reports from an electioneering pamphlet onwards ascribed to Cicero's brother, but more probably an exercise of the Augustan period, that the versions are combined. Given this disparity, there is a case for acquitting Catiline of this particular charge, and, as we shall see, of the killing of a distinguished brother-in-law. In 64 he was to face prosecution by Lucceius for other murders of the Sullan terror, and Lucceius, friend of Cicero, may have included the charge. However, Cicero himself, a kinsman of Gratidianus, though of uncertain degree, had been thinking of collaborating with Catiline in 65 and never later mentioned the murder of Gratidianus. This is the strongest evidence in Catiline's favour.

There are other victims. Q. Caecilius, or Caucilius, named by Cicero and the pamphlet, is likewise said to have been Catiline's brother-in-law, an elderly man uninvolved in politics (he may be

Plutarch's 'brother'). If we took Gratidianus into account, it would look as if Catiline was going for his wealthy equestrian kinsmen by marriage, men chosen by his father to reinforce the family fortunes. Caecilius' name appeared on the Sullan proscription lists, and it was easy to charge Catiline with using that to cover a private crime. It is tempting to believe in the murders or denunciations of other knights, unpolitical, but evidently monied: M. Volumnius and L. Tanusius mentioned in the election speech; the pamphlet adds Titinii and Nannei. Nothing could have been better calculated to blacken Catiline in the eyes of surviving Marians and their sympathizers, especially members of the equestrian order. However, the charges brought against Catiline in 64 were never properly tested; he was discharged, at the instance of the presiding judge – Caesar. The valuable Catiline's political career was saved. Modern scholars have mounted effective defences; others, remembering modern political atrocities, are less sceptical.

Catiline, 30 years old in 78, was qualified to hold the quaestorship in that year, that of M. Lepidus' consulship and revolt. Nothing is heard of him, but he may well have followed Pompey's example, shunning the rebel. No man who came out of the Sullan revolution with his fortunes enhanced, as Catiline did, could avoid bitter resentment. But it was not until 73 that Catiline was first attacked – which also suggests that he may have been absent from Rome since his quaestorship, perhaps in Spain fighting under Pompey.

The offence brought out by Sallust was of incest in the Roman sense, and extremely serious: intercourse with one of the Vestal Virgins who tended the eternal flame in Rome. This was a capital offence, way beyond accusations of adultery or fornication with unmarried women of the nobility. Men and women had died for it 40 years before, the women by burial alive after two increasingly severe trials. It was in 114–13, when invading Germanic tribes appeared. In 73 there was fear from the rising of Spartacus, and Mithridates was

26 *Catiline*

still a force in the east. The Vestal involved with Catiline was Fabia, a woman of distinguished family and half-sister or cousin to Cicero's wife Terentia. M. Licinius Crassus was also accused, with the Vestal Licinia. Crassus was a follower of Sulla, but not known for cruelty, and certainly not for licentiousness, only for greed and devious politics. Indeed, his (acceptable) defence, according to Plutarch, was that his meetings with Licinia concerned an estate of hers that he was trying to buy. Catiline and Fabia also escaped. Q. Catulus, the loyalist consul of 78 and son of Gratidianus' victim, pontifex (high priest) and perhaps president of the court, may have persuaded his fellow pontiffs to acquit, defeating the plebeian accuser Plotius. (A namesake was to bring in a Lex Plotia for the return of Lepidus' followers and a reforming agrarian proposal in 70.) Certainly Catiline in 63 gave thanks to Catulus for help in 'severe dangers' and it looks as if M. Cato, descendant of the great Censor, induced the formidable young patrician P. Clodius Pulcher to give up haranguing the people for a retrial, as had happened in 113.

The question is why the still comparatively insignificant Catiline was brought before this rarefied tribunal. In 114–13 the main target had been women of the highest rank, including another Licinia; the dominant clan of the time, the Metelli, were under fire, though the paramours had been mere knights. 73 was a good occasion for a theatrical replay of 114–13, with Spartacus still a force, Mithridates VI resurgent, a grain shortage, tribunes declaring themselves powerless against the nobility, and political turmoil in the aftermath of the Sullan settlement at a peak. The accusers were attacking a spectacular target for *populares*, the iniquity that was causing Rome's problems. As to Catiline, the murders perpetrated by his Gauls were well known. The nobility closed ranks. Crassus proceeded in 72 to the war against Spartacus, and it may be that the charge was designed to prevent him winning the command. It was a trial balloon. The Vestals were not going to be buried alive (the regulation penalty), nor

Crassus and Catiline beaten to death with rods. His career proceeded with the help of distinguished men, and he marched on towards the praetorship. All the same, if the claim is true that only 25 per cent of senators of this period were now facing public trial during their careers, Catiline was attracting more than usual attention.

Other sexual offences are specified (the *Pamphlet on Electioneering* graphically offers 'violating young boys almost in the lap of their parents'). But Catiline's marital history is lurid enough. He had two, possibly three wives. If we accept that he slaughtered his wife's brother Gratidianus in the Sullan revolution, his first marriage was to Gratidianus' sister. Yet this element of the Gratidianus story has also been challenged. The evidence for that marriage comes from the Berne Scholiast on Lucan's *Pharsalia*. B. Marshall in his commentary on Asconius concludes that the Scholiast has run together the two murders, of Gratidianus and Caecilius, ascribing the connexion with Caecilius to Gratidianus. With 'Gratidia' dismissed, the name of Catiline's first wife is unknown.

The second was the focus of a more elaborate and even more lurid story. Catiline had made away with his first wife, Cicero implied in 63 BC – refusing to go on to another 'unbelievable crime'. Evidently the facts were that she was succeeded (perhaps with haste, to give the story of murder some credibility) by the high-born and wealthy Aurelia Orestilla, a connexion of Cn. Aufidius Orestes, consul in 71 BC. She was a woman for whom Sallust grimly claims that no decent man had anything to say, except about her beauty. The story further went that Orestilla was unwilling to accept Catiline's proposal because he had a grown son and heir in his house, a threatening stepson. This problem was solved when the young man died, reportedly murdered (specifically by poison, according to the moralist Valerius Maximus) by Catiline; Sallust implies however that the initiative lay with Orestilla. Not only that; Catiline's bride was his own daughter from a previous liaison, with a young unmarried girl of 'noble' birth (so of a consular family), still unidentified, which according to Cicero and Plutarch resulted in the birth of the daughter whom Catiline subsequently married. The mortality rate in the ancient world, notably in malaria-stricken Rome, was cruelly high and Catiline was never brought to court for the murders; the varied elaboration of the stories shows them up as embroidered fictions.

When the marriage to Orestilla took place is unclear; this was not Orestilla's first, for she too had a child, a daughter. The mid-sixties have been urged, for in 64 the tribune who vetoed the senate's proposed anti-bribery measure, which is thought to have been aimed at Catiline and his running-mate, was a Q. Mucius Orestinus, probably adopted from the Aurelii. This date provides only a *terminus ante quem,* but alliance between Catiline and Orestinus offers another reason for rejecting the story of Catiline's marriage to his own illegitimate daughter – a woman accepted as a member of Orestinus' house, when she was potentially a disgrace to it and its *paterfamilias.*

However, Catiline faced a worse obstacle to this career than his Sullan past, the crimes of his Gauls, and the scandals of his private life. Riches came from Sulla's proscriptions, but Catiline allegedly dissipated his on luxury. Roman 'luxury' was a matter of competitive display, essential in the political game; hence the laws passed against it. It was likely then that, as Appian explicitly claims, it was ambition that reduced Catiline to poverty. He was buying his way into increasingly costly office, the quaestorship (20 places now), the praetorship. Men and women were still courting him, and he will have made them gifts, or at least promises. So Catiline was successful for the praetorship of 68. He was not to know that with this office his legitimate career had already reached its pinnacle. To follow the magistracy, he was allocated the governorship of the province of Africa. The quip was that a governor needed to take home three fortunes, one to pay off his creditors, one to buy off the jury if he were prosecuted, and one for himself. Complaints against Catiline were reaching Rome even while he was still in Africa, to be deplored in the House – but welcomed by critics and rivals for the next post. When he laid down his *imperium* on his return, he would be prosecuted and, if convicted, would lose profits and political career, perhaps life in Rome.

Catiline on campaign and on trial

But while Catiline was fleecing the Africans a scandal broke at Rome that gave him a hope of reaching the consulship of 65, to which a praetor of 68 was entitled, instead of 64, and so of evading formal indictment. The successful candidates in the elections of 66, P. Autronius and P. Cornelius Sulla, a relative of the late Dictator and beneficiary of his proscriptions, were unseated for electoral bribery under a statute brought in by the optimate consul, C. Calpurnius Piso, in the previous year. Another election would be held, and Catiline decided to stand. With Sulla out of play, L. Manlius Torquatus, one of the defeated candidates, was the only patrician that Catiline would have to beat; his other rivals were all plebeians. The consul who was presiding over the elections, L. Volcatius Tullus, is not known for any prejudice against Catiline. It may have been constitutional propriety, and the advice of the advisory council mentioned by Asconius, that made him declare that he would not take account of any votes cast for Catiline in the supplementary election.

The explanation provided by Sallust is not lucid. He claims that the candidate, who was having to face a trial for extortion ('*repetundarum reus*'), had not been able to declare himself a candidate within the legally required period ('*intra legitumos dies*'). But Catiline was not yet formally on trial, and it is not clear whether the period mentioned by Sallust means the period before which candidates must declare their candidature (three market days, which occurred every nine days) in the first election, which Catiline had missed, or the second. (Candidates usually spent far longer than three market days on the canvass. Cicero, for example, began his campaign a year before the poll, in July 65.) It seems best to follow H. R. Dietsch's edition in rejecting the phrase about Catiline's inability to declare his candidature in time as a knowing comment that has crept into the text. It was his status as a potential defendant, probably pressure from friends of the Africans, and some dislike of Catiline in high places, that blocked his candidature.

Catiline took the refusal quietly, stopped canvassing, and underwent his trial for extortion. Cicero told his friend Atticus that he would be acquitted – 'if the sun does not shine at mid-day'. Apparently it did not. Again Catiline had distinguished men on his side, including the successful candidate for the replacement consulship, Torquatus himself, as his legal adviser. Other consulars spoke for him as character witnesses. The prosecutor, an earlier antagonist, P. Clodius Pulcher, had allowed supporters of Catiline on to the jury. Despite his conviction of Catiline's guilt, Cicero thought of supporting the defence: if Catiline were acquitted he could be a partner in the elections of 64, when Cicero would be standing. In the end he must have thought that helping Catiline would only add to his own opponents, and he took no part in the case.

The acquittal did not come in time for Catiline to become a candidate for the consulship of 64, but it left him free to try for 63. Coffers were replenished, perhaps by further loans, which would have to be repaid if he were successful and proceeded to a rich province. He was now a strong candidate. As he was a patrician, any running mate would have to be a plebeian, as at least one consul of the year must be. Cicero even considered joining forces with him, but again drew back. Catiline's past, and his popular sympathies, perhaps the source of his funding, were attracting hostility from conservative circles. According to Sallust he enjoyed the discreet support of Caesar and Crassus, and Cicero could not afford that: they were big men, envied and feared by their peers in the Senate. He was to take quite a different tack. In the end Catiline allied himself with M. Antonius, another candidate of radical sympathies. Cicero's speech on his rivals has to be reconstructed from Asconius' commentary on it: Catiline and Antonius were backed by a noble who was using massive bribery to offset their ill repute. They had no regard for institutions or for Cicero himself. If bribery failed, they were ready to use runaway shepherds or hired gladiators. Catiline was the heavyweight: he had offended leading men of the state, senators, knights, and plebs. Then came the moral outrages and the fictional 'first Catilinarian conspiracy', its aim the slaughter of optimates (see below). At most we can conclude that the beginnings of Catiline's more radical programme were appearing. It is said that after one meeting in Catiline's house there was a fall on the exchange, and it was only an injection of cash by the banker Q. Considius that checked it. As to his backers, Asconius too names Crassus and Caesar: that was what Cicero claimed later in his political memoirs. Of the candidates on offer, Catiline might well seem the most effective and pliable. Indeed he may have had other wealthy backers – the disgraced P.Sulla was flush with money. But Cicero may have *known* nothing: the object was to blacken his rival and frighten respectable voters. So Catiline failed to win the consulship of 63, though Cicero had to accept his fellow plebeian Antonius as a colleague in a polarized year when debt and resentment made change and reform imminent.

A mere prick compared with this defeat was the charge of murder brought against Catiline by Lucceius just after the election. Yet it demonstrated that he still had friends as well as enemies: the support of consulars helped bring about his acquittal, or rather the abandonment of the case by the judge appointed, Julius Caesar; Lucceius was reduced to publishing his prosecution speeches. The defeat and the trial show Catiline pivoting from his Sullan past into the *popularis* role in which, he was to proclaim in the Senate House and then claim to his faithful friend Q. Catulus, 'I followed my usual custom in taking up the general cause of the unfortunate'. That cause in 65–63 looked like winning, and Catiline backed it. By now his own difficulties made his thinking grateful to the poor:

> It is impossible for anyone faithfully to defend the poor except a man who himself is as poor as they are. Men in an embarrassed and desperate condition ought not to trust the promises of the rich and powerful, and therefore, those who wish to recover their possessions should take note of the man who claims to lead them of what his own losses are, of what still remains to him and of what he dares to do. The leader of the dispossessed must himself be dispossessed and also very fearless.

Julius Caesar the *popularis*

The early careers of the three young men who served at Asculum offer a good way of triangulating the possibilities for men entering political life in the 80s. However, they were all superficially at least on the winning side, that of Sulla and the champions of senatorial supremacy. Gaius Julius Caesar, born in 100 BC, Cicero's equal as a literary man, Pompey's superior as a soldier, offers a contrast: he was *popularis* from the start and had a vertiginous career accordingly. By birth he had claims to distinction beyond those of the patrician Catiline: Caesar's clan came by way of Iulus, son of Aeneas, from the goddess Venus, Aeneas' mother. But his direct forebears had little success to show. However, his family allied itself with a wealthy and influential politician: Caesar's aunt Julia was the wife of Gaius Marius, and in the mid-80s Caesar was closely connected with the dominant 'Marian' clique; he was married to Cornelia, daughter of its leader L. Cornelius Cinna. When Sulla took over, Caesar, the story goes, was invited to divorce Cornelia and look elsewhere for a spouse. He refused and was put in danger of his life. This story would have enhanced his credentials when antipathy to the restored senatorial oligarchy took on strength. More credible was the tale that he was intended for the post of Flamen Dialis, a patrician priesthood of Jupiter that was so set about with taboos – for example, about absence from Rome and contact with corpses – that it made political and military life impossible.

In the 60s he was even more obvious. He put on games in memory of his long-dead aunt Julia, parading his Marian connexions. He supported bills that gave Pompey his commands, and the restitution of rights to the sons of men proscribed by Sulla. As aedile (a magistrate who regulated Rome's markets) in 65 he canvassed for the grant of citizenship for Gauls north of the Po. Aristocratic birth had brought him another prestigious priesthood early in life: the pontificate. In 63, the same year that he was elected to the praetorship, he stood for the post of Pontifex Maximus, head of that priesthood, against strong opposition from a veteran member of the oligarchy, Q. Catulus. At 37, Caesar was a stripling by contrast, and when he won in the tribal assembly that further inflamed the anger of his enemies. Borrowing money against his future success abroad, Caesar left for Spain and for campaigns that allowed him to seek a Triumph on his return. This was refused by the Senate on the grounds that he was a candidate for the consulship of 59 and could not stand 'in absence', that is, while he was waiting for his Triumph outside the sacred boundary of Rome. By now Caesar had as many optimate enemies as Pompey. Ancestral pride made him as determined as Catiline to reach the consulship and beyond, but he was cleverer and more consistent, took decisive and unmistakable action, had superabundant charm, and evidently easier access to credit (he looked like a winner); and he was innocent of crimes committed in the 80s. He was attacked in malicious sexual gossip as virulent as what was spread against

Catiline: serial adulteries, and when he was on service in the east in 80, a liaison with Nicomedes King of Bithynia, and one in which he particularly disgracefully played the passive role – a man for all women and a woman for all men. Accusations of womanizing were not always hostile: Caesar's own soldiers warned citizens of Rome to lock up their wives when they returned home in triumph in 47 with their commander, the 'bald adulterer'. Catiline allegedly took a lover with him when he left for Etruria in 63, Tongillus by name, along with Publicius and Munatius, two men who could not meet their bar bills. Passive homosexuality (the serious charge), could not be proved against him.

4

Catiline's 'First Conspiracy', 66–64

The threatened outbreak of violence, 66–65

Beyond the underlying conditions, blame for the explosive state of Rome and Italy in the 60s lies at the door of senatorial politicians, as jealous as a century before of any individual who might win the credit of relieving the problems of any group, such as the indebted, and the wealthy equestrians who feared loss of capital and profit; while the mass of people at Rome would have felt their usual reluctance to share the privileges of full Roman citizenship with Caesar's Transpadanes.

In the city itself violence, unrest, and talk of revolution were endemic. Politicians and historians seized on hot contemporary rumours and developed them for their own purposes. In particular, one series of episodes has been worked up into what has become known as the 'first Catilinarian conspiracy'. We have seen Catiline, despite a vulnerable reputation, pursuing a conventional career, but in 66–65, three years before he left Rome and joined forces with the insurrection in Etruria, he was already involved in another plot to assassinate consuls and take power. So it was alleged.

As we have seen, the consuls elected for 65, P. Autronius Paetus and P. Cornelius Sulla, had their election annulled, and Catiline's bid to replace Sulla failed. At the turn of 66–65 there were disturbances in the Forum and rumours of worse, principally involving the unseated consuls designate; Sallust categorically declares that this constituted an attack on the Republic. The nub of the story was that these men meant to assassinate the new consuls of 65 who had supplanted them, L. Aurelius and L. Manlius Torquatus – who had shared the praetorship in 68 with Sulla and Autronius and spent a year as a legate of Pompey – on the first day of their year of office. In the developed version of the story that Sallust gives, the established villain, Catiline, has replaced Sulla. Furthermore, the developed story went, when the conspirators were in charge at Rome, they were going to send a young man called Cn. Calpurnius Piso as quaestor to Hither Spain to secure the province. Unfortunately the plan became known, so that action was postponed for three weeks, to 5 February, with an augmented scheme of assassinating several senators. This second endeavour was thwarted because Catiline gave the signal too early.

Not only was this story, and its imaginative variants, something for any ancient politician or historical writer to work up according to his own interpretation of events; modern writers have brought out as many interpretations of what happened as there are papers on the subject. It was R. Seager who brilliantly deconstructed the entire farrago as a series of puppet shows, its variants developed from one politician or writer to another, according to need. It was Cicero who involved Catiline, as early as 64, and used the story to back up his attack on him in 63, when the first Catilinarian speech has him standing armed in the Forum on 29 December 66, apparently in a grotesque rehearsal for the assassinations to take place on the following day. In 62 Cicero had to exonerate P. Sulla, his client in one of the crop of cases that followed the exposure of the main conspiracy in 63. By then Catiline was a player available for a leading role in any conspiracy story. From Cicero, the story of Catiline's involvement passed to Sallust, Livy and Cassius Dio. Unusually, Caesar's biographer Suetonius has nothing of Catiline here, but contents himself with Autronius and Sulla, backed by Crassus and Caesar. One stock *popularis* is substituted for another, giving more prominence to the protagonist of Suetonius' biography. In fact, the alleged victim Torquatus acted as defence counsel at Catiline's extortion trial in 65 – unlikely if he had been the target of a murderous 'Catilinarian' conspiracy. It is entertaining to recall that on his own account Cicero in 65 thought of supporting Catiline's defence team, with the idea of a joint candidature for the consulship.

The tribune C. Manilius and the quaestor Piso in Spain

A more substantial player in the scenarios of 66–65 was C. Manilius, whose tribunician bill of 66 had conferred the command against Mithridates on Pompey. The optimates did not forgive him, and he was immediately prosecuted for misappropriation of public funds. The trial should have begun in 66, within the last few days of December, but Cicero, who as praetor was presiding over the court, and had originally granted Manilius only one day to prepare his defence, did not proceed. The trial was postponed until the next year. Indeed, when it came on, under the new praetor, Cicero, who had delivered a speech in favour of Manilius' bill, defended him (but not successfully). If Catiline did appear armed in the Forum at the end of December 66 it was to demonstrate in favour of Manilius – and that was enough for the incoming consuls to win a bodyguard from the Senate.

In his election address of 64 Cicero expanded the 'first Catilinarian conspiracy' to accuse his rival Cotta, with the conveniently deceased Cn. Piso, of a grand 'massacre of the optimates', and exploited the same story in his defence of Murena at the end of 63. For Piso was indeed sent to Hither Spain, a mere quaestor with a praetor's *imperium* to neutralize the powerful influence of Pompey, who had created ties of patronage with the inhabitants during his campaigns there. Piso was soon assassinated on the road by Spanish cavalrymen among his troops, and that made the theory even more attractive, especially as it could be asserted that he had been sent there with the help of the plutocratic Crassus' influence. Crassus' support for the appointment was evidently open – he urged it in the House. Not all commentators believed that the assassins were partisans of Pompey; some attributed the murder to resentment that Piso's own conduct caused among Spaniards. Sallust is surprised by this: they had borne worse in the past. He declines to choose one view or the other. The finger was pointed at Pompeian sympathizers, but an inexperienced commander in rough country was well able to bring about his own death without help from Crassus' jealous rival. Well into the Principate another Calpurnius Piso met the same fate in Spain.

For Sallust, intent on making a coherent narrative, Catiline's defeat in 64 merely marked a step forward in the development of an existing conspiracy: practical measures were taken, the collection of weapons at suitable points in Italy, the conveyance of borrowed funds to the Sullan centurion C. Manlius at Faesulae in Etruria, making him an initiator of the rising. More adherents were drawn in, including women who had previously paid for their extravagance by prostitution but who, as beauty faded, had fallen into huge debt (presumably now by pawning their jewels). Appian also comments on the number of women who financed Catiline – he claims because they wanted to murder their husbands; it is evident that they were dissatisfied with their status and freedoms.

Catiline nonetheless decided to stand again for the consulship in 63. Sallust's preparations for revolution on his part, potential rebels in Rome and Italy, were only political supporters for him at this stage. He could expect opposition to his election from the presiding consul Cicero and would use whatever weapons came to hand to neutralize him.

How Cicero was elected to the consulship in 64

Unrest and the promise of further reforms of the Sullan dispensation, such as the return to the sons of the Sullan exiles of their property and political rights – anathema and a source of fear to senators in possession – help to explain how Cicero, for all his flirtations with populism and his friendship with Pompey, came to be elected consul. He worked hard at the canvass, touring the cities of northern Italy, but confessed to his friend Atticus that he was detested by the nobility. Not only his politics but his ignoble birth made him both despised and suspect. Atticus will have turned to and reassured his own aristocratic friends, consulars such as Q. Hortensius, L. Lucullus, L. Torquatus, and men destined for the heights, M. Cato and Q. Caepio Brutus, that Cicero was a man to trust, clever and strong enough to deliver security during his term of office and afterwards. This solid son of Arpinum would not support the radical social measures that were being mooted, especially if there were any threat of violence.

In other words, a bargain, tacit or explicit, was struck between Cicero and a section of the nobles. In return for the longed-for consulship, he was to take on supremely dangerous tasks: thwarting the reformers and the populace, repressing any consequent violence. Furthermore, the job had to be done quickly, without provoking a premature rebellion, before Pompey should return from the east; otherwise there would be an obvious case for asking him, with his highly trained and experienced army, to put the insurrection down. That would leave him in just as good a position as he had been in 71, when he returned and trod out the embers of Spartacus' revolt. Another irregular consulship such as that of 70, and within ten years of the last, was a political nightmare for the optimates. He might even demand a Dictatorship.

When Pompey would return was uncertain. Sixty-three, the year of Mithridates' death, would have been possible, but after wintering in Antioch (Antakya) Pompey became involved in Judaea and captured Jerusalem only after a three-month siege ending towards the beginning of October in that very year. Pompey arrived at Brundisium (Brindisi) towards the end of 62, when the revolt was all over.

It was this bargain, then, together with his oratorical skill, his previous successes and the grateful clients they brought him, and an impression of 'provincial' steadiness, along with the undesirability of his needy competitors Catiline and M. Antonius, that brought Cicero in at the head of the poll – although the undesirable Antonius was also elected. In an unpublished paper on the events of 63, the political historian C. E. Stevens cited a saying of the American senator Boies Penrose: 'A good politician is one who, having been bought, stays bought'. He cited it in connexion with Caesar's relations with Pompey, but it is just as apposite for Cicero's relations with the optimate oligarchs. His services to them meant that he stayed bought: he had nowhere else to go. The question remains what oligarchy feared most, and what the relationship was between Catiline, the conspirators executed by Cicero at Rome, unrest in the city, and the uprisings in Italy.

5

The Catilinarian Conspiracy of 63

Cicero's province

When consuls took office they knew what provinces the Senate had allocated to them for the year after they laid it down. The consular provinces declared for 62 were Macedonia, where a governor had fine chances of warfare followed by a Triumph, and Cisalpine Gaul. The lot brought Macedonia to Cicero, but at some point he offered it to his colleague Antonius, buying his compliance in Cicero's actions as consul and, rumour had it, a share in Antonius' profits from Macedonia. Cicero himself did not go to a province at all until new arrangements compelled him to take Cilicia in 51, for he went on to cede Cisalpine Gaul to the praetor Q. Metellus Celer (consul in 60). If necessary, both Celer and even Antonius could be called upon to put down disturbances in Italy. And there was a sound general, Q. Metellus Creticus (consul in 69), waiting outside Rome with segments of his army for the Senate to grant him his Triumph; he was available for Apulia. As we have seen, Cicero's education did not make him a military man; and that would be a consideration in this year. The province was hardly a sacrifice for such a city animal. Others much greater would be demanded.

Cicero and the radicals: The Rullan bill

Cicero, and his oratorical powers, were soon put to the test. He had to deliver on the undertakings he had given to thwart *popularis* radicalism. This had clear implications for Catiline, who was now to make his third bid for the consulship at the July elections of 63. On 10 December, before Cicero came into office at the beginning of the year, a new board of ten tribunes of the plebs took over, several of them dangerous radicals. They tried variously to restore political rights to the sons of the men proscribed by Sulla, to mitigate or cancel the punishment imposed on Autronius and Sulla for the misconduct in the elections of 66, and to cancel debt. We know most of the purposefully unkempt P. Servilius Rullus, whose project was a far-reaching bill, backed by his colleagues, that would distribute public land to individual settlers, even precious land in rich Campania, found colonies, and buy further plots for distribution out of the sale of other public property in Italy and the provinces. But it had wider aims: to reaffirm the title to ownership of the Sullan settlers, who had had it under challenge since 81 and could not sell because their uncertain title kept the price down; likewise to reassure Sulla's colonists, who could not sell or mortgage because their titles were under threat. In other words, it would have done even more than what Julius Caesar's consular land bill was to do four years later.

But Cicero attacked the bill in the Senate and before the people, with threats of death against anyone who disturbed the status quo. Some attacks were to appeal to the propertied class, others to the ordinary people of Rome; he focused on the loss of revenues to the state that disposing of public land – particularly the cherished Campanian lands (Ager Campanus and Ager Stellas), destined for 5,000 settlers – would mean. He could claim as well that the bill favoured the poor of Italy against the Roman plebs, and that

The Catilinarian Conspiracy of 63   43

unprivileged settlers would be sent to unattractive and distant sites, while the 5,000 country colonists would soon have their allotments bought up by rich men from Cumae (Cuma) and Puteoli (Pozzuoli). This attacked two plebeian targets at once, rustics and rich. Beneficiaries would be 'restive, ready for violence, prepared for sedition'. The composition of the ten-man board ('kings', Cicero offensively called them) who would supervise the distributions was another target. Besides, the board would exclude Pompey, who was still abroad campaigning and would be unable to stand for election in person, as the bill required. So he was able to argue that the bill was aimed against a popular hero. It lost impetus and seems never to have been put to the vote. The crushing of the Rullan bill might lead to disturbances but Cicero took the risk: he would put them down. In January he had laid the foundations for his great achievement of December.

The trial of Rabirius and the assassination of *populares*

Another indication of the current wind direction came when a man was indicted for the murder of politicians in a riot of 37 years previously. The victims were L. Appuleius Saturninus, a tribune of the plebs and therefore sacrosanct, and C. Servilius Glaucia, praetor. These were the leading *popularis* politicians of the late second century, the successors of the Gracchi and allied to Gaius Marius. In 100 Marius was consul for the sixth time and Saturninus was passing legislation to provide his discharged soldiers with land. They needed more time and sought immediate election to further office. A murderous act of their followers led to street fighting. They holed up in the Senate House, but Marius could not prevent a mob from climbing onto the roof and killing his former allies with tiles torn from it. Now in 63 the tribune Titus Labienus, whose uncle had also died in 100, on a wave of *popularis* feeling brought to book one of the leaders of the mob, the aged senator C. Rabirius, on a charge of high treason, which carried a grisly death penalty to be imposed by the two-man board set up to try him.

Rabirius appealed to the People against the antique procedure that Labienus was invoking and Cicero and the optimate Q. Hortensius came out in Rabirius' defence in his subsequent capital trial in the assembly. Caesar, who had been appointed judge with his kinsman Lucius, allowed the charge to drop. These were *popularis* manoeuvres; during the trial Cicero was able to claim that there was no thought of fighting: he saw no weaponry; there was no violence or murder; the Capitol and Arx were not under siege. But the *populares* had made their point: the danger to anyone who violated the sacrosanctity of a tribune of the plebs.

Labienus had another popular proposal for 63, again in association with Caesar: he transferred the election of priests from the Sullan system of co-optation by existing members of the colleges to popular election by a section of the tribal assembly. At the end of the year Caesar was rewarded for his popular stance by being elected Pontifex Maximus (leading pontiff). Sixty-three was a year in which popular aspirations for change were in the air, although there is no reason for supposing that all *populares* were acting together: they were all bidding on their own behalf and could become rivals.

Whatever the fate of the programmes that 'reforming' politicians put forward in 63, hankering for change and unrest were emerging more and more clearly among the people in Rome and Italy. This was different from the personal squabbles that went to make up the 'first Catilinarian conspiracy'. Whatever plotting, if any, one accepts for 66–65, it concerned only Roman politicians. No mass movement or even partisans from the countryside were involved. It was quite different for the movement of 63, in which the defeat of social reform and candidates who advocated it would lead to further pressure, perhaps violent, from the dispossessed at Rome, throughout Italy, and abroad.

The people of Rome and Italy in 63

There is a vehement claim from Sallust that the entire mass of the people at Rome, the plebs, supported revolution, and that only Cicero's warning that the conspirators intended to burn the city down swung them against it. Two of Cicero's published Catilinarian speeches, the second and third, were addressed to the people, one to inform them that Catiline had left Rome, the other to claim that the conspirators had confessed. Their hopes and anger had been aroused by the *popularis* tenor of the tribunes of the year. Piracy and long-drawn-out war in Asia Minor had raised prices. Settlement in colonies allegedly in distant and infertile places proved unattractive. Debt reduction or abolition was another aspiration for those who owed rent on their apartments, or food or bar bills. The masses were not homogeneous: landlords, even those who were subletting a room, and the owners of food shops and pubs wanted their accounts settled. They themselves might be in debt, if they were renting; and if they were freedmen their property might revert on their deaths to the family of their patrons, leaving their children destitute. Political sentiment heated up the underprivileged: Caesar's prosecution of Rabirius reminded them of how their champions might be annihilated, and interspersed in the crowd were slaves who had nothing to lose and everything to gain – loot, freedom – from chaos.

One might ask now what the consul was doing to relieve the hardships and political grievances of his fellow Romans. The answer is: nothing. Cicero knew that debt had reached a new level during his consulship, as he wrote himself. His response was to send a quaestor,

P. Vatinius, to Puteoli (Pozzuoli) to prevent the export of gold. Cicero had nothing positive to offer; even minor reform would be construed as betrayal of the optimate cause by an unreliable instrument and an attempt to win credit for himself. But radical candidates for 62 could only benefit from his unbending opposition.

There were murmurs elsewhere than at Rome, and widespread evidence provides a formidable list, from north to south, of places and peoples outside Rome that were actually or potentially involved in the risings of 63 and so available to subversive elite leaders. As far as Italy was concerned, the configuration of unrest was notably similar to that of the Social War.

In October eventually came irrefutable news (perhaps welcome to Cicero) of an armed uprising in Etruria, focused on Faesulae (Fiesole), one of Sulla's veteran colonies, and neighbouring districts. Arretium (Arezzo), 60 kilometres to the south, was also restive and, rallying to Manlius, the area was 'armed' by Catiline, as Sallust claims, trained perhaps by experienced ex-officers.

The genuine grievances of such colonists were shared, or rather redoubled, by the men they had displaced. Like the Umbrians, the Etruscans had been slow to join the other allies in the war against Rome in 91; consequently they had speedily been rewarded with the Roman citizenship under the Lex Julia of late 90. The author of that bill was a connexion of Marius, who took refuge in Etruria when he fled Rome in 88. Besides being culturally and linguistically distinct, Etruria had suffered particularly severely from Sulla's confiscations, and in 78 it had been involved in the rising of Lepidus. The leader of the revolt in 63 was a Sullan centurion, Manlius, who had lost the wealth he had won in the Civil Wars; by contrast the standard to which his troops ultimately rallied had belonged to the Marian army. Two separate strands of discontent were unified and made the core of the insurrection. It was a Faesulan from the colony who was in charge of the left wing in Catiline's last stand.

From north to south a wide range of writers, from Cicero down to Orosius, attest to the other areas affected:

1. In Transalpine and Cisalpine Gaul there were disturbances at the time of the rebellion in Etruria. Already C. Piso, consul in 67 and governor of Cisalpine and Transalpine Gaul 66–65, is mentioned as subduing a revolt of the Allobroges (around Vienna [Vienne]). Currently they were still suffering from debt and a renewed revolt was only put down with difficulty in 62 by a praetorian governor, C. Pomptinus. The Ambrones of Liguria and the Gauls north of the Po were also restive.

2. Picenum in north-east Italy: Catiline sent his henchman Septimius here, and other agents to Picenum and elsewhere; there were disturbances at the time of the rising and the praetor Q. Metellus Celer was authorized by the Senate to take stern measures, including raising troops in Picenum and Cisalpine Gaul. A Picene equestrian magnate involved in the conspiracy was L.Vettius, who was another tiro on Pompeius Strabo's advisory council in 88; he informed on the conspiracy. Antonius' quaestor P. Sestius dealt with C. Mevulanus, a junior officer of M. Antonius and an abettor of the conspiracy at Pisaurum (Pesaro) and in the Ager Gallicus, and with C. Marcellus, a leader among the Paeligni.

3. Umbria, bordering on Picenum: the conspirator Septimius was a native of the city of Camerinum (Camerino).

4. Latium: Aefulan territory, north of Praeneste (Palestrina): with the revolt under way, Catiline moved there with his army, intending to seize it: Praeneste had been the site of the younger Marius' last stand in 82; the citizens were massacred by Sulla and a colony established in the territory.

5. Campania: Capua was a centre of gladiatorial schools and armaments factories. It had a history of secession, factionalism

and unsuccessful attempts at colonization, proposed again in Rullus' land bill. It was the source of Spartacus' original band of escaped gladiators; now a new insurrection threatened and P. Sestius the quaestor, after working in Capua and Rome, joined Antonius in Etruria. At Pompeii the original inhabitants were at loggerheads with Sullan colonists; naturally they favoured Catiline, and allegedly were being egged on by P. Sulla.

6. In the Apennines: in the Paelignian territory rumours of a slave revolt were dealt with in 62.

7. Samnium: the Samnites had fought Rome in a series of bitter wars, rose again in the Social War and had been the longest to resist; Sulla gave his veterans individual grants in the area.

8. Lucania: in the instep of Italy the Lucanians had joined the Samnites against Rome in 91, and held out with them. Their condition did not improve as a result.

9. Apulia (Puglie), a country of pastoralists in the heel of Italy, gave rise to rumours of an uprising; C. Julius and M. Caeparius of Tarracina (Terracina) were to go to Apulia and rouse the slaves. There was a threat of division of public lands under Rullus' bill, and Q. Metellus Creticus was sent to defend it.

10. Bruttium (Calabria), the toe of Italy: there were disturbances at the time of the rising, with tension at Thurii (Thurio) between locals and Sullan veterans. The Emperor Augustus' father C. Octavius, who was on his way in 60 to govern Macedonia, under senatorial instruction won a success near Thurii against remnants of Spartacus' runaway slave force and of Catiline's levies in southern Italy. Octavius' son was named 'Thurinus' from this success. A minor but spectacular participant in the conspiracy, Volturcius, came from Croton (Crotone), though Cortona in Etruria has plausibly been suggested as an emendation to Sallust's text.

This list shows that what thanks to Cicero and Sallust came to be called the 'Catilinarian conspiracy' was a widespread reality with deep roots and became a genuine threat to the stability of the oligarchical government and to established social structure. It does not always tell how serious these movements were, how they were interrelated, and how closely, if at all, they were connected with elite plots at Rome. It looks as if the movement of C. Manlius was autonomous; others were local responses to promises of reform and debts of loyalty called in by superiors, copycats of neighbouring movements, or desperate acts of opportunism. They need not have been Catilinarian at all, but Manlius at least, with his voting power, will have been in touch with Catiline throughout his campaign for the consulship, and sent as many of his men as could afford it to Rome to take part in the voting. With such voters Catiline was doubly damned in the eyes of the oligarchs. Supporters will have drifted home after the elections, to congregate round Manlius as they realized that nothing would be done for them. It was a paradoxical combination, but all wanted a clear and secure settlement. When we are told that Catiline 'sent' henchmen to an area, it may mean that these were local men returning from the failed elections.

The resources of the oligarchy

The ruling oligarchy was not unprepared or unarmed. Italy itself contained no garrison. But the legions of generals returned from abroad and awaiting triumphs were encamped in it, and Cisalpine Gaul had a permanent garrison. Between 67 and 65 both the Gauls, Cisalpine and Transalpine, were under the conservative C. Piso, consul of 67. By 63 four legions were divided between the two provinces. Besides these forces the consul had at his disposal subordinate magistrates, the quaestors, and his own private resources of slaves and freedmen, as well as those that his political allies were willing to lend him.

Cicero would have been negligent to ignore the violence that was in the air from the beginning of the year. He himself boasts of his vigilance and its success. Slow as communications were, he will have had information from friendly landowners throughout Italy, always the backbone of his 'army', from patriotic merchants travelling into the provinces, especially Gaul, from his own spies – his slaves or freedmen, or men in his pay. Informers and men who tried on prosecutions on their own account were a constant factor in Roman history, for policing was a hit-or-miss affair. At Rome, too, there were young men itching for a role in politics and kept out of significant magistracies until they were 30, sons of senators and intrinsically unsympathetic to the masses. They might enjoy intimidating them and even taking part in a brawl.

Catiline's candidature of 63

Now, with a tide of popular feeling behind him, Catiline made his final bid for the consulship. His candidature had once been refused, and he had been defeated in 64, in part through Cicero's efforts – and now Cicero was consul and presiding over the current election. Yet Catiline had his loyal and influential friends, the revered Q. Catulus among them. As a candidate for the highest office in 63 he was not a lost cause. What happened after his final defeat has misled ancient writers such as Sallust into antedating the conspiracy by a year, Appian into claiming that for him the consulship was only a step towards tyranny. So far, Catiline was after conventional prizes, the material rewards that an ex-consul's governorship could bring, and the prestigious seat among the consular senators that he would enjoy for the rest of his life. His radical noises may not have been taken

The Catilinarian Conspiracy of 63

51

seriously by experienced and sceptical politicians. He had sympathizers in the Senate too, men whose own finances would not support a successful career. And he had wealthy backers (Crassus' is always the name that comes up) who would find him useful once in office. Cicero had to work hard.

According to Dio Cassius, it was with Catiline in mind that Cicero passed the law against electoral misconduct mooted in 64, strengthening the Lex Calpurnia that C. Piso promoted in 67: the penalty became ten years' exile. In this last canvass Catiline was offering the cancellation of debts (*tabulae novae*, 'fresh accounts'), one of the most radical measures that any Roman politician could propose in that society of cash shortage and high interest rates. In the campaign of 64 he is said to have been supported by Crassus and Caesar; but the prospect of cancellation of debts should have put off Crassus. Crassus was in a difficult position in 63. To modest inherited wealth and his practice at the bar he had added by exploiting his private fire brigade. If that were unsuccessful in saving a building, he would buy the remains at a bargain price and rebuild with the prospect of profitable rents. Besides that, he had added to his wealth by money-lending among senators, who became politically indebted to him as well for the continuation of their careers. Allegedly these debtors included Caesar and Catiline, and would naturally have included some whose indebtedness was attributed to extravagance or immorality. Crassus was not trusted or liked, but his complex web of relationships made him vulnerable to change, and quietude was his natural aim.

Sallust includes in what he still presents as an electoral harangue promises not only of the abolition of debt but proscriptions of the wealthy (a dreaded word since Sulla), magistracies, priesthoods, looting and all the privileges that attended a successful insurrection. Either Catiline's or more probably Sallust's imagination was carried away. Catiline also had on his side, in the same account, the presence of Piso in Spain and of a P. Sittius in Mauretania, with armed forces.

But Piso hardly survived until 63 and Sittius, who joined Caesar's movement in 49, was still an innocuous businessman, exonerated by Cicero in his defence of P. Sulla in 62.

As the plum of his account of Catiline's speech to his supporters, Sallust relates how they took an oath sealed in bowls of human blood mixed with wine. This indispensable ingredient of any conspiracy worth the name – of which Cicero in his first speech against Catiline apparently knows nothing, since he simply wonders whether the sword intended for his own assassination may have been hallowed in some way – cannot belong here before the elections; how conspirators later chose to pledge their faith is another matter. Sallust himself, suspending judgement, allows the possibility that lurid charges such as this were thought up by those who were hoping to help Cicero escape the anger that he aroused by executing Roman citizens without trial.

Until July, then, Catiline was merely a candidate for office, but he was accused of threatening a rival, the legal expert Servius Sulpicius Rufus, and was to be prosecuted by the stern moralist and supporter of senatorial government M. Porcius Cato. Cicero postponed the elections on the grounds of possible violence. They were discussed in the House over two days but the Senate, which contained sceptics, enemies of Cicero, Catiline's influential connexions, and his hard-up sympathizers, let them take place after a delay, whether of days or – as has also been proposed – until Cicero was presiding again in September. Catiline found himself summoned before the House by Cicero to explain his revolutionary remarks and this was the occasion for a notorious declaration: 'There are two Romes, one thin and wasted, with a weak head, the other strong, but as yet without a head.' The allusion was to the Senate and Cicero and to the populace and some unnamed individual – Catiline, or Pompey. It was true enough and so alarming. The Senate groaned and could do nothing. Some were afraid to make their mark and be noticed. As C. E.

The Catilinarian Conspiracy of 63   53

Stevens observed, some senior members remembered the uprising of M. Lepidus in 77: Q. Marcius Philippus reminded senators, after the event, how few had voted for action against him. Catiline stalked triumphantly out of the House.

At the elections Cicero let it be seen that he was wearing a breastplate under his toga, a precaution that the Emperor Augustus was to take when he was tampering with the composition of the Senate. Violence, even a massacre threatened, Cicero insisted. It did not materialize, but the threat was used in the following year by P. Sulla's enemies to implicate him in the Catilinarian conspiracy. We are free to see Cicero's imagination at work – and being turned against him when Sulla was put on trial. But the election result, however achieved, was satisfactory for Cicero: the successful candidates were L. Licinius Murena, a man who had been legate to L. Licinius Lucullus in the war against Mithridates and was supported at the election by Lucullus' veterans, and Decimus Iunius Silanus.

In December – still in the midst of the Italian insurrection and the hue and cry over the conspirators at Rome – Murena was put on trial for electoral bribery; such were the preoccupations of minor Rome politicians even at moments of crisis. Another defeated candidate, the jurisconsult Sulpicius Rufus, brought the charge, along with Cato. Sulpicius had his grievance, and it was probably justified, if Cato supported the charge at a time when, as Cicero argued in his defence of the incoming consul, Rome rather than a lawyer needed all the loyal generals she could get. He did not say that they would be even more useful if such generals came from the camp of Pompey's enemy Lucullus, but merely insisted that it was essential that there should be two consuls to usher in 62. At any rate, Cicero and Q. Hortensius, with Crassus not surprisingly in support, convinced the jury, all men of property, and Murena went on to take office on 1 January.

From politics to conspiracy: Catiline and his allies

The dashing of legitimate hopes intensified the despair and anger of have-nots throughout Italy, besides creating a potential leader for them in the failed candidate. It was after his failure at the election of 63 that Catiline, in Cassius Dio's crisp narrative, entered on the conspiracy. After the final defeat Catiline was finished as a politician, for success after three failed attempts on the consulship was exceptional: Q. Lutatius Catulus had succeeded for 102 only with the help of Marius. In 63 rioting followed, presumably from Catiline's supporters, and he and his ally Cornelius Cethegus were threatened, as the news arrived from Etruria, with prosecution for electoral violence by L. Aemilius Paullus, son of the insurgent of 77. As an act of bravado, the accused Catiline took up residence with the praetor Metellus Celer (Cicero having refused custody of him). In any case Catiline would have found his creditors pressing for payment. The choices were suicide, bankruptcy and social death, reasonably comfortable exile among provincials impressed by the presence of a Roman senator, and a violent coup. He looked round among his friends, and took stock of the situation in Italy.

Sallust provides a classified list of Catiline's friends, but gives it at the point when Catiline was still a candidate in 64, prematurely damning them all as conspirators and already assigning them specific roles. Some were longstanding associates or allies. Beyond any such list there must have been a train of loyal dependants: slaves, freedmen, clients, whose names are unknown; members of the hired gangs, such as P. Clodius Pulcher deployed so effectively in the following decade.

The question is how closely the urban conspirators were connected with Catiline in any case. Are they to be seen as subordinates, or as members of one or more other groups that thought of exploiting unrest in Italy and Gaul? Sallust has four classes. The first is of

The Catilinarian Conspiracy of 63   55

senators, some with prime roles in the plot. P. Cornelius Lentulus Sura, a ringleader at Rome, was a man reputedly idle, even lethargic. In spite of an early disgrace incurred as quaestor in 81 under Sulla, he had risen to the consulship of 71, only to be expelled from the Senate in the following year. The censors responsible for this clearance of 64 men were pro-Pompeian, but had their own judgement to follow. They had left Catiline alone. In 64 Sura had been elected praetor again, so regaining his status as a senator. One has to ask then whether status was all he wanted. A rewarding province, and another consulship perhaps, but as a second-time-round candidate he will not have stood a good chance for a post offering only two vacancies a year. Otherwise why risk everything in the conspiracy of 63? (Cicero's colleague in 63 was another man who had lost his place in 70, but Antonius had never previously risen higher than the praetorship.) In a sense Catiline and Lentulus Sura would be rivals in revolution rather than partners. Another patrician, C. Cornelius Cethegus (often bracketed with Sura as a leader, and portrayed both by Cicero and Sallust as a reckless desperado crushed by debt) met his death in 63. It is not surprising that the elder Seneca (c. 54 BC–AD 39) described the Catilinarian conspiracy as a 'patrician crime'. Some of its leaders shared with Sulla and Caesar a strong sense of what was due to their rank.

P. Autronius Paetus we have already encountered in 66–5: a consul designate unseated for bribery, and so perhaps also expelled from the Senate along with P. Sulla and L. Vargunteius, whom Cicero implicates in the disorder of 66. In 63 all three escaped death but they were prosecuted in the following year on a charge of affray. (A new law against such violence may have been passed in the mid-60s.) L. Cassius Longinus, a stout party and a would-be arsonist according to Cicero, also escaped in 63, the year of his own failed attempt on the consulship, to be convicted in 62 on the same charge as Paetus. Another P. Sulla, and his brother Servius, were the sons of Servius

Sulla, clearly kin of the Dictator and of the unseated consul designate; they went the same way. The role assigned to Q. Annius Chilo by the ringleaders – or by Cicero – was liaison with the Gallic tribe, the Allobroges. M. Porcius Laeca, in whose house the conspirators met, was another target of retribution in 62. Towards the end of his list, Sallust includes L. Calpurnius Bestia. This was the tribune of 62 who assailed Cicero for executing Roman citizens without due trial. He escaped, as tribune designate since the elections of 63, then as tribune since 10 December, and so formally untouchable. The odium that would have attended the execution of a tribune designate was too great to be risked. The shades of the Gracchi and their political heirs protected Bestia, though not from verbal abuse.

Sallust then lists four knights, surprisingly, given the wealth and political quietism associated with the rank, until it is remembered that men expelled from the Senate reverted to equestrian status. Some men on Sallust's list of senators probably belong to this category, notably Q. Curius, who turned state's evidence. His increasingly boastful and brutal conduct towards his cooling mistress, the noble Fulvia (he would soon be the master, he thought), caused her to relate everything she had heard to a considerable number of people, without mentioning Curius; or, according to Diodorus, to Cicero's wife Terentia. That, evidently, was enough to bring Curius to the optimate side, though Caesar succeeded in depriving him of any rewards. The other equestrians on Sallust's list were M. Fulvius Nobilior, who, if the name forms a genuine part of the text, may be identical with the senator's son killed by his father for taking part in the conspiracy, and seemingly kin to Fulvia; yet another C. Cornelius, from the plebeian branch of the clan, allegedly the companion of Vargunteius in an abortive attempt on Cicero's life; L. Statilius (would-be arsonist); and P. Gabinius Capito (charged with liaising with the Allobroges), both executed. Last come unnamed leading men from the country towns of Italy, the 'nobility' of their own cities,

The Catilinarian Conspiracy of 63   57

many of them enfranchised in the Social War and still subject to the prejudices of their betters. Only under the Principate were they to come into their own as senators and equestrian functionaries.

Of the two women among Sallust's *dramatis personae,* Fulvia and Sempronia, Fulvia had a real part to play as Curius' mistress, the typically female role of go-between; Sempronia seems to be brought on simply for Sallust to luxuriate in disapproval of her accomplishments and the impropriety of her masculine behaviour. Besides, Sempronia was the mother of M. Brutus, one of Caesar's assassins, and so was of interest at Sallust's time of writing. A tiny addition may be made; Sempronia and Fulvia bear names that belong to families with strong *popularis* connexions: Gaius Sempronius Gracchus, the tribune of 123–21, was the loyal ally of M. Fulvius Flaccus, consul 125 and tribune 122; they died together, along with Fulvius' son. Family tradition, real or fancied, may have guided the later women in their choice of political associates. Florus calls Fulvia a bargain-basement whore, but that has nothing to do with her social status. Twelve years after the conspiracy of 63 Fulvia is placed by a moralizing author, Valerius Maximus, in a brothel party with the consul Metellus Scipio, organized by one of Scipio's official attendants. The details may be fiction, the background is convincing.

Depravity of the conspirators

In Sallust's view, the associates were all moral reprobates: debauchees, gluttons, and gamblers who had squandered their patrimony; those who had had to buy legal immunity; men convicted or murder or sacrilege, or who feared conviction; perjurers and assassins of their fellow Romans; all who were being driven by criminality, poverty or a bad conscience were Catiline's closest friends. Sallust seals his case by insisting that if any blameless person did form a friendship with

Catiline he was soon corrupted. It is remarkable, too, how strongly Sallust insists on Catiline's cultivation of the young, presenting them with the gifts that would be most welcome to each: prostitutes, dogs or horses. He is not at all certain that the young men who frequented Catiline's were there for sexual purposes; there was no evidence for it. This might give greater credence to his other allegations – as perhaps he knew. Certainly the young, dependent on their father's generosity, were plausible targets for a politician's attention when debt reduction was part of the programme. But, as E. Isayeva has insisted, Catiline had to woo his acolytes, and they were won by his charisma, not by youth ideology. Fear of parricide fascinated the Roman paterfamilias; the law provided a special penalty for those who committed it, that of being sewn up in a sack with wild animals and thrown into the sea or a river. But Sallust fails to provide a satisfactory explanation of the financial desperation of the age. The core Italian economy, its climate and fertility, failed to provide for the manpower needed to sustain the Roman political ambitions, and the wealthier classes were developing a taste for luxury.

The problem of debt

Debt ran right through Roman society, as we have seen, and was a torment to small shoppers and drinkers with a tab, tenants, to enterprising merchantmen, to farmers with plots they could not sell such as the colonists settled by Sulla the Dictator, to all farmers and landowners rich in property and poor in cash, to young men unable to touch the inheritance they expected from their father, and to all aspiring politicians stretched by the competitiveness of the post-Sullan political scene. Those who had been able to amass capital in cash, generals and their troops on campaign abroad, 'successful' provincial governors and the 'publicans' who took on from the state

The collection of taxes, privately lent out what spare they had, or invested it in property for rent. Among the masses, debt reduction was a vote-winner, but the centuriate assembly was dominated by voting blocks of the wealthy and frightened; they could distribute bribes and apply patronal pressure.

Connexions between the urban conspirators and their social inferiors were easy to establish; both sides would have been keen to provide mutual assistance: men with large town houses (Catiline left Rome with 300 men) or estates in the country well provided by labour from men formerly under their military command. Shepherds and runaway slaves could not hope for redress; they could only flock to an uprising, take available loot, and hope to fade away afterwards. So they had flocked to Spartacus in the late seventies. But representatives of the unhappy colonists in Etruria and elsewhere, who in Sallust's hostile view had squandered their bounty and longed for another civil war, and of the men whose land they had received, could certainly have made their way to Rome in the pre-election period and promised support at the hustings. All over Italy, bodies of electoral supporters became a patchwork of insurrectionists.

The insurrection in Etruria

Manlius did not mean to stay near Faesulae and hope that the Senate would voluntarily initiate legislation that would relieve his followers of debt or secure their property. While the Senate 'negotiated' and drummed up troops for punitive action, Manlius' own forces could drift away. He needed to march on Rome and make a more forceful leverage. Yet a mere ex-centurion, authoritative as he might be in a legion, in which there were 60 such officers, was lower in rank than a knight and nothing compared with members of the House. The marchers needed a leader of a higher class; a senator of praetorian rank would do. It had always been an obvious tactic for Manlius to make contact with sympathetic politicians at Rome in the hope that they might win concessions by peaceful means – it might just as well be the current praetor Cornelius Sura as the would-be consul, especially after Catiline's failure.

At the same time Manlius, with scant regard for any revolutionary allies he had in Rome – he may well have regarded the failed consular candidate as a spent force – sent representatives to Q. Marcius Rex (consul 68), one of two generals conveniently waiting with troops outside Rome for a Triumph; he was on the Via Cassia. The delegates protested that Manlius and his men had only taken up arms out of desperation at their destitute state. The letter reproduced by Sallust may well be authentic, if Marcius recorded it in his dispatches to the Senate. Moneylenders and the urban praetor responsible for regulating them were to blame. There had been earlier concessions by the Senate, notably the Lex Valeria of 86 (during the 'Marian' supremacy), which allowed debtors off three-quarters of their debts. And the ruling class had let the hateful bill pass. The letter further recalled three historic 'secessions of the plebs' that had taken place in the fifth and third centuries BC: in a kind of strike, the people, politically oppressed by the patricians, had withdrawn from the city to nearby strong-points. All Manlius and his followers wanted, he claimed, was protection from moneylenders – that is, extended credit and low interest rates. Marcius prevaricated; he could not make concessions – he would have to consult the Senate – and he demanded that the rebels disband and present themselves at Rome as suppliants.

Q. Arrius, an ex-praetor, brought news of the impending movement to Rome on 21 October; the revolt finally broke six days later. How does revolt break out? By refusal to pay tax, as in Boston in 1776; by refusal to admit representatives of higher authority, or violence towards them, as at Asculum in 91; at Faesulae literally by the raising of military standards – that is, by the illegal creation of irregular forces. It was a clear-cut moment.

Declaration of tumultus and the SCU

The Senate declared a state of emergency known as a *tumultus*: a threat of violence against the state was taken to justify any civilian in taking up arms and donning military dress. Successful commanders of unimpeachable background and political views were instructed to deal with the outbreaks in Faesulae and Apulia, Q. Marcius Rex and Q. Metellus Creticus; to Capua and Picenum praetors were dispatched: Q. Pompeius Rufus and Q. Metellus Celer, on his way to the province of Cisalpine Gaul – both were of unspotted optimate credentials. They had *imperium* and were given permission to hold a levy. Troops of gladiators were to be distributed between Capua and other country towns, according to their resources. Capua, to which the quaestor P. Sestius was sent, seems a strange choice, given the disturbances reported there, but training schools and barracks were well manned, and presumably, since Spartacus' outbreak, with armed keepers. The declaration of a *tumultus* and the instructions given to commanders show that the Senate took the unrest seriously. The orders they received cannot have come solely from the consul, though there was permission to hold a levy: troops for Antonius to take to Etruria.

More news was to come. Within a few days a senator called L. Saenius read out a letter to the House informing it that Manlius and a large force had actually taken up arms on 28 October. Along with a crop of portents and prodigies, the House heard of other rallies and assemblages of weapons: a slave revolt was breaking out at Capua and in Apulia. L. Aemilius Lepidus, younger son of the consul of 78 (he needed political respectability) had already begun to moot proceedings against Catiline and possibly Cethegus on a charge of stirring up violence. But legal procedures were overtaken by events. Catiline's ostentatious efforts to put himself into the custody of Cicero were rebuffed; he had to be content with a Caecilius Metellus as warder.

The Senate's response to the danger at Rome and in Italy by passing the so-called 'Ultimate Decree' has been discussed at length in scholarly literature. The decree required the consuls and other office-holders 'to ensure that the Republic came to no harm', a directive that had first been passed in 121 against the supporters of C. Gracchus. Legally, it meant nothing: it was presumed that the consuls were normally intent precisely on ensuring the safety of the Republic. It was rather a political measure, promising the officials support if they exceeded their authority or infringed the law, and its value depended on the strength of will of the Senate. How useful it was to Cicero in 63–62 will be discussed below.

The action taken by the Senate against dissidents in Italy, which entitles scholars to see it as a momentous crisis, can be set against their hesitancy in taking measures against conspiracy at Rome, and that supports the view that they thought that they were dealing with two separate phenomena and were even oblivious of any urban conspiracy. Early in November Cicero enlightened them. A reward of 200,000 sesterces and impunity were offered to those who gave information if they were free, freedom and 100,000 for slaves. The free men envisaged would have been low in rank, to be tempted by such a modest reward. Watchmen were to be posted throughout Rome, organized by junior magistrates. Sallust paints the city population as stricken, men and women in a panic. The women, in this stereotypical scenario (it was only when the world was falling apart that they could express themselves so freely), struck at themselves, stretching out their hands to heaven and begging mercy for their children, asked continual questions, and trembled at everything, forgetting their usual arrogance and vanity.

Setting the conspiracy in motion: The letters delivered to Crassus

Some time after the election, then, on the received account, Catiline had 'sent' his supporters into promising areas and made contact with potential rebels. At Rome preparations continued for arson and assassination, according to Sallust, with suspicious vagueness; at any rate they did not come to anything. It is in Cicero's first speech against Catiline (8 November), when Catiline was still in Rome – actually in the House – that we hear of the military standard despatched to Manlius in Etruria. That may be a later insertion.

When the panic over the unrest in Italy was at its height, a packet of anonymous letters addressed to politicians, including the resonantly named Q. Pius Scipio and M. Claudius Marcellus, optimate consuls of 52 and 51 and so perhaps quaestors in 63, was delivered to Crassus' house. Crassus passed them on to the consul in the night. Cicero summoned the Senate the following morning. Crassus' letter was read out. It warned of bloodshed, a massacre on 28 October. Cicero passed the letters on to their addressees. This was a bizarre episode. Who wrote the letters and delivered them? Crassus' disclosure did not eliminate his reputation as a backer of *populares*, a former friend of Catiline, and so a man with a foot in two camps. After his death in 53, Cicero accused Crassus of backing Catiline, a charge easily made and impossible to rebut. That reputation precisely may be the reason for the letters being deposited on him. Conspirators might think that their letters would stigmatize him as a sympathizer. If he kept quiet about them they could publicize the fact that they existed and were with him; if he revealed them to the Senate they would still show how he had been regarded by some in the conspiracy – whom he was now betraying. More simply, the letters were an insurance policy for conspirators with consciences, who would lay claim to them if their plans failed. More simply still, they were Ciceronian forgeries, a plant that the eminent ex-consul would have to take to the Senate (Crassus would know that there would be copies if he destroyed them). That would add immense weight to Cicero's claim of a dangerous conspiracy. That is the preferable solution, avoiding the hypothesis of simultaneous multiple confessions. Cicero benefited, and comes under suspicion.

The date appointed for the massacre in the letters passed without incident. Then Catiline summoned his leading confederates for a dressing-down. On 6 November they met at the house of P. Porcius Laeca and he reported all he had done. For further progress, the assassination of the stalwart Cicero must come first. That proposal threw the others into confusion, but two men who had been expelled from the Senate, C. Cornelius (taken for Cethegus in some writers) and L. Vargunteius, promised to do the work by making a 'morning call' on Cicero on 7 November and stabbing him to death. Fortunately the informer, Q. Curius, who may have hoped to find his salvation by serving the state, was present and was able to use his mistress Fulvia to warn the consul (the means of communication seems strangely elaborate). Cornelius and Vargunteius were refused admission to the house, creating a disturbance in their attempt.

Like the firing of Rome, this was one of the features of the plot that suspiciously failed to come off. The meeting itself has been treated by some scholars as an outright fiction, part of Cicero's construction of a monstrous plot to overthrow senatorial government, plausible once Catiline had left Rome. Nonetheless, there is enough substance in the story of a meeting for it to produce any number of damning and false elaborations. Up to the time of the rising in Etruria, men still refused to believe in Cicero's Catilinarian conspiracy; the meeting linked the two branches. Assassination was a known political weapon at Rome: the murder of the tribune Livius Drusus in his own house in 91 had led to the Social War, and in 66–65 it was plausible to envisage

The Catilinarian Conspiracy of 63   65

a pair of desperadoes assassinating the consuls and seizing power; rumours about the possible assassination of Pompey frightened him into staying indoors in the early fifties. Less than 20 years after the Catilinarian conspiracy, 63 men succeeded in killing Julius Caesar, and for a while their leaders remained more or less in control of Rome. The planned attack of Vargunteius following on the meeting may have been no more than a fiction of Cicero's, but it would carry some conviction.

Catiline's departure from Rome

Catiline's activities were suspect, and L. Aemilius Paulus' attempt to arraign him under the Lex Plautia against affray was the legal course in the circumstances; it was under that law that other alleged conspirators were tried in the following year. But arraignment took time, and before anything could come of Paulus' proceedings, Cicero on 7 November summoned the Senate to the temple of Jupiter Stator, the god who stays Roman defeats, and in the face of Catiline himself launched his attack. He was planning to assassinate the consuls and to overthrow senatorial government. Cicero could now even supply chapter and verse: the 'morning call' from Catiline's henchmen and its rowdy outcome. Many of Cicero's audience were sympathetic, keen to get rid of Catiline and all his kind, or frightened of revolution. Some were sceptical, aware of Cicero's obligations to the optimates and unconvinced by his evidence. According to Diodorus, Cicero could not extract an answer from the Senate on the question as to whether he should banish Catiline (consuls could relegate men to a limit of 100 miles from Rome), and Catiline himself declared that he would not go into exile without a trial.

At this point Sallust allows Catiline to be heard, though in indirect speech. Catiline spoke of his noble birth, his ancestors' services, and his own. 'Is it possible to believe that a patrician like myself, the product of such a race, should wish to destroy the Republic, or that it should be saved by an immigrant, practically a lodger in Rome?' Before he could say any more, senators shouted him down, as an enemy of the people and a murderer. Cicero's speech produced an audible effect, then, showing Catiline how few senators openly sided with him; he may well have come to believe that if he stayed in Rome there was nothing he could do to save himself from Paulus' prosecution and its propertied jurymen. Scholars have asked why Catiline did not reply to specific accusations – about the meeting at Laeca's house, for example. But it was a question of interpretation: the visit was one thing; what went on there was another matter. Sallust gives Catiline's last enraged words in the House: 'My enemies have destroyed me. I'm being driven out. I'll bring down the building and put out the fire that way.' With that he rushed out of the temple. Fine words, but Catiline used them when Cato threatened him with prosecution before the elections: 'If a fire is set to my destiny, I shall put it out, not with water but by pulling down the building.' Perhaps Catiline found it too good to waste. Having decided to leave at once, according to Sallust he told Lentulus Sura, Cethegus, and his other associates to do what they could to bring on fire and insurrection.

It is natural to hold that Cicero intended to drive Catiline out, as Catiline claimed, and to force him to declare his hand. The first speech against Catiline has the consul summing up the situation just before a formal debate began: Catiline has asked to be referred to the Senate and to have the Senate pronounce its opinion on him. That, not surprisingly, was denied him.

The attempted assassination took pride of place. In its published form the speech gives the impression that Catiline was being urged to leave – for his own sake, seeing that he was an enemy of the Roman People who deserved to die. 'Catiline, leave the city, deliver the Republic from its terrors. Be gone into exile, if that is the word you are waiting for.' Silence. 'You see, Catiline. They heard me and are silent. Why do you wish to hear their voice banish you when you can tell their feeling by their silence?' Cicero is only uncertain whether he was right to let him go. However, it remains possible that that was not its aim, but that Cicero would have preferred to take all the conspirators at Rome together. Yet he lacked evidence, and the Senate was divided. So the outcome of the speech was favourable to Cicero: at least Catiline was gone into exile, admitting political defeat; by joining Manlius he would make himself manifestly guilty of treason. On the other hand, some scholars have believed that Catiline intended to leave Rome before Cicero ever spoke, whether to go into exile or to take control of the movement in Etruria. Cicero was only snatching the credit for driving him out. When he addressed the people afterwards, he was still uncertain what he had achieved: 'At last we have thrown Catiline out of the city, or driven him out, or, when he was leaving of his own accord we have pursued him with words.'

Exile or rebel?

When Catiline went north, he made as if he were going into exile at Massilia (Marseille) a free city of Greek foundation, and always a favourite with exiles (C. Verres was already there). On the route he dispatched messages to a large number of men of consular rank and others of high standing. He claimed that it was false accusations that had brought him down. He was yielding to the inevitable and going to exile. He had no sense of guilt, but wanted the state to be at peace, with no unrest arising on his account. On the other hand his personal and longstanding friend, Q. Catulus, read a letter out in the Senate which was more revealing:

Your extraordinary loyalty to me, which I know from experience, is welcome to me in my grave dangers and gives me confidence in commending myself to you. For that reason I have taken a fresh course of action and decided not to prepare a defence. It is not from any sense of guilt that I am offering an explanation; heaven knows you are aware of the truth of it. I have been stung by wrongs and insults and, deprived of the fruit of my toil and hard work, was not winning the position that belonged to my rank; so I have done as I have often done before, taken up the cause of the deprived wherever they are. It is not that I couldn't pay off my own debts from my own property (and the generosity of Orestilla would pay off with her own and her daughter's money debts that have been incurred through others); but I have seen unworthy men raised to honour and office, while I felt myself become an outcast through unfounded suspicion. It is on this account that I have taken up hopes, honourable enough in my circumstances, of preserving what remains of my dignity. I should like to write more, but news has come that violence is to be used against me. Now I commend Orestilla to you and entrust her to your loyalty. See that you protect her from insult, in the name of your children.

Whatever Catiline wrote to other senators, he and his train of 300 (armed, of course, and including his friend Tongillus) were prepared for other goals than exile. They were carrying symbols of Roman authority, rods and axes, fully deployed as the insignia of a consul on arrival at Faesulae. Figures of the number of men involved differ from one author to another (and when the number of men killed in battle are concerned, fluctuations are particularly wild). A force of 2,000 men, half of them fully armed, was probably what Catiline found when he reached Etruria. His efforts and present charisma were enough to raise them to 12,000 (two legions' worth, a quarter armed), though their maximum conjectured strength was 20,000 men, a quarter fully armed (so Appian). When the final battle came, after the executions at Rome, they may well have fallen to 3,000. Cicero had cruel words for this force: 'Desperate old men, dissipated clowns and ignorant spendthrifts, men who had broken their bail to join the uprising. It will collapse if I send not an army drawn up in line of battle but simply a warrant from the praetor.'

All the same, a stirring speech, and Catiline had evidently taken command. Up to his departure he may have been uncertain what to do. For his route north to Massilia he should have taken the coastal Via Aurelia but may rather have chosen the Cassia into Etruria, or have left the Aurelia at Forum Aurelii (Montalto di Castro) to spend a few days with his associate C. Flaminius at Arretium. This is the last moment for the letter to Catulus, ambiguous as it is, and seemingly composed at Rome, for it is the last moment for Catiline to make up his mind to join Manlius. That he should keep his options open was obvious, in case the revolt collapsed. News of the decision strengthened Cicero's position immeasurably. He had already harangued the people in his 'Second Catilinarian' of 9 November and told them that their *popularis* champion had fled.

Cicero without his villain

Cicero's immediate task was to bring as many of the populace as he could behind the forces of law and order. On 9 November he addressed the people in the Forum, and informed them of other facets of the conspiracy, particularly of the fact that, as the consul was assassinated in his house, the conspirators were allegedly to set fire to Rome at several sites. This, according to Sallust, turned them decisively against the conspirators. Not only were the forces of law and order, such as survived, to be thrown into confusion – the cancellation of debts and the overthrow of one consul in favour of another established by violence they might welcome or view with equanimity – but the burning over their heads of the apartment blocks where they kept their families and their only possessions was something quite different. They had experienced that as the result of casual sparks and always would, despite the efforts of emperors to organize fire brigades and strengthen building regulations in the city. Purposeful arson was not to be borne.

About nine days after Cicero delivered that second Catilinarian speech, his victim was declared an open enemy of the Roman People (*hostis*) – something that came much more easily when a man had left Rome and might attack it like a foreign enemy. Virtually a consul at Faesulae, Catiline was an enemy of the people at Rome. Cicero would now have been in a position to make a clean sweep of malcontents in Rome itself and to intimidate slaves and the destitute free – if only he had concrete evidence against them. As to Italy, information came readily into his hands. It was the urban conspirators who needed to be decisively exposed. According to Sallust, Cicero induced Fulvia and Curius to keep him informed of the progress of the conspiracy. Large sums of money must have changed hands, even without the later official rewards. But Cicero needed more, and it providentially turned up early in December.

Catiline's rival at Rome

To the five men executed in the Tullianum dungeon and the others he lists, Sallust adds shadowy figures: Roman nobles, men of consular descent, with no poverty or other compelling reason for involvement; they simply wanted a monopoly of political power. He also mentions restless youths of the nobility, bored with a quiet life. These would have been the opposite numbers of young men recruited by Cicero. Much more significantly, he mentions the suspicion that attached to M. Licinius Crassus, Pompey's colleague in 70 and now his bitter rival. Crassus (so runs the story, still current) was fully aware how tense the social and economic situation was in Rome and Italy by the beginning of 63. He feared Pompey's army and hoped to build up a counter-force from whatever source he could. This is fantasy. Revolution and counter-revolution would be catastrophic for his business interests, as it would have been at the time of the 'first conspiracy'. Peace and security, achieved by adroit manoeuvring, were what he needed.

The most prominent of the conspirators at Rome was actually P. Cornelius Lentulus Sura, the praetor of 63, another descendant of an ancient patrician family. It was unlikely that he would be elected consul for the second time when competition was so intense and he had already once been discredited. We do not know either what province he would have been allocated after his current praetorship. Pompey's successes in the east and his reorganization made it unlikely to be very profitable. His own alleged plan for Rome in its fullest reported form, ripening after the departure of Catiline, was to massacre the Senate, seize the children of Pompey as hostages, and burn the city through the agency of 100 men divided between the districts, while others cut the aqueducts. As praetor, with Cicero dead and Antonius bought, he would be a in a good position to take power on his own account.

With Catiline's departure the 'Catilinarian conspiracy' falls apart, in spite of Cicero's attempts to create a unity out of it. The letter that was eventually produced to establish the guilt of the two leaders is telling: Lentulus wrote to Catiline giving him instructions. He was not second in any scheme dominated by Catiline, but regarded himself as an equal or superior. Cicero quotes the letter and Sallust claims to reproduce a copy of it; I print the former version:

> Who I am you'll know from the man I have sent to you. See that you play the man, and think about the position you have reached. Consider what you must do now. Take care to bring over help from everyone, even the lowest.

To these instructions Lentulus added an oral message: seeing that Catiline had been declared a public enemy by the Senate, what did he think he was doing to refuse slaves? Everything he had ordered in the city was ready; he shouldn't hesitate to come nearer the walls himself.

The first sentence of the letter is coy about Lentulus' identity, and this has caused difficulties. Catiline should have known Lentulus' well-known seal and his handwriting if they were familiars in the conspiracy – hence a reason for disjoining the two movements, linked only from this time forward. This does not necessarily follow: the coyness was a clumsy attempt at maintaining security. The transaction shows two independent enterprises collaborating. Lentulus hoped that the threat from Catiline and Manlius would create such a panic at Rome that his own plan could be realized; he meant to use them.

Even more importantly, the letter issues instructions that were expressly rejected by Catiline. He is told to seek help 'even from the lowest', that is, from slaves. It was one of Catiline's redeeming features, in the eyes of quiet citizens, that he never did that, except perhaps at the last. Catiline's 'cause' was one for Roman citizens. He meant to take over the government from Etruria, not to overturn the entire basis of Roman society, which depended on slavery. That was what made the rebellion of Spartacus so terrifying as he rampaged through Italy with his gladiators and runaways.

Nor did the activities of Catiline and Manlius in Etruria chime in well with those of the conspirators at Rome. Each group was waiting for decisive action from the other, afraid to act without being able to count on active support from the others. Even the conspirators at Rome were not united. According to Sallust, Lentulus and his associates planned to deliver a popular attack on Cicero in a formal public speech to the people to be delivered by the incoming tribune of the plebs, L. Calpurnius Bestia, whose term began on 10 December. That was to be the signal for the actions planned for the following night; but we are also told that they were planned for a day of the Saturnalia Festival, which began on 17 December, when houses were conveniently left open all night to receive gifts. As public speeches were not allowed that day, it seems that action must have been postponed to a day or two after that – hence the headstrong Cethegus' protests against delay. The plans were, allegedly, the dozen arson attacks by Statilius and Gabinius and their followers, while this time Cethegus was to batter at Cicero's front door and attack him; youths, especially of the nobility, were to murder their fathers. With the city in confusion, there was to be a mass exit to join Catiline. The story went that even these plans were not enough for Cethegus, who was savagely violent and ready for action; in his impatience he promised an attack on the Senate House. The plan for Bestia's inflammatory speech is plausible, but the details of the actions to follow look like a compilation from Cicero's box of theatrical tricks, with the threatened mass exit another attempt to unify the conspiracies. Cicero still needed convincing evidence to achieve that for him. He was lucky.

The Allobroges to the rescue

Cicero, with Catiline indisputably mired in the rising in Etruria, was looking now to arrest the leading troublemakers at Rome. For this he found the ideal instrument: two ambassadors of the southern Gallic tribe of the Allobroges, who were in Rome to enlist help against the grasping operations of Roman financiers. The Allobroges were one of the most powerful tribes of southern Gaul, rich in manpower as well as in possessions, but now, it seems, unbearably in debt. They would have spent heavily on the Roman amenities that became available when their territory was included in the province of Transalpine Gaul, especially after Pompey had intervened in the area in the

74 *Catiline*

seventies. Not a penny changed hands there, says Cicero, without the involvement of Roman citizens. Upon any new or reorganized province there also descended a swarm of tax collectors, whose profits depended on what they could extract from landowners, travelling merchants, and the like. Republic and Empire alike provide examples of provinces taken over and soon in rebellion, with excessive taxation given as the cause. The Allobroges, with their delegation to Rome, looked for an innocuous remedy, at least in the first instance. They hoped for help from influential Romans, in particular from the man described by Sallust as their patron, Fabius Sanga.

Naturally the Allobroges were watched. They consulted their patron at Rome, and he reported to the consul. Cicero prepared a trap. But we are also told that they were themselves solicited by the conspirators. Lentulus sent the freedman P. Umbrenus, who was known to them from business deals, to accost the envoys in the Forum and offer them the help that the Senate had evidently refused. Umbrenus took them to the house of D. Brutus; he was away, but evidently Sempronia was about. Cicero's story was that the ambassadors got themselves introduced to the other conspirators by Gabinius and demanded a written and sealed oath from them promising redress (Lentulus Sura, Cethegus, Statilius and Cassius are specifically named), which they could take back to their fellow tribesmen in southern Gaul; only Cassius avoided taking the oath and left Rome before the delegation. Lentulus sent a man called T. Volturcius so that he could bring the ambassadors to Catiline and confirm the alliance, entrusting Volturcius with his peremptory letter to Catiline. Together with Gabinius, Umbrenus gave the Gauls a list of participants, but tried to impress them more by inserting the names of men who had nothing to do with the conspiracy. If all this is true, we need to ask what they were required to do in return. There can be only one answer: aid a revolution in Rome and Italy by providing a distraction in the province; however it was put, it meant an open refusal to pay their debts and the expulsion or murder of Roman officials – even the supply of troops, especially cavalry, for which the Gauls were famous, to the rebel army.

When the night for the Gauls' departure was fixed, 3 December, Cicero, thoroughly well instructed by the delegates, ordered two loyal praetors, L. Valerius Flaccus and C. Pomptinus, experienced military men, to arrest them as they crossed the Mulvian bridge that carried the Via Flaminia over the Tiber north from Rome. The Allobroges surrendered at once. Cicero's men seized letters addressed by the conspirators Lentulus Sura, Cornelius Cethegus and L. Statilius to the Allobrogian capital Vienna (Vienne), and captured the messenger T. Volturcius. Volturcius resisted at first, appealed for help from Pomptinus, whom he knew, then surrendered.

At dawn Cicero summoned the letter-writers and Gabinius. He sent a praetor to the house of Cethegus and, not surprisingly, uncovered a collection of weapons. With this evidence in hand, Cicero called the Senate to a meeting in the Temple of Concord. Volturcius was brought in first, and, offered a pardon, claimed to be a recent recruit to the conspiracy. He amplified his evidence, incriminating Gabinius and Caeparius; he had heard Gabinius mentioning, among others, P. Autronius, Ser. Sulla and L. Vargunteius as participants. His instructions from Lentulus had been to push Catiline into recruiting slaves for an immediate march on Rome, where the city conspirators would have caused panic with their scheme of fire-raising and assassination.

Volturcius' evidence was then corroborated by the Gauls in a separate examination before the Senate. They named the ex-praetor Cassius and confirmed that the city was to be fired; they even had a date, 17 December, the Saturnalia (which does not jibe well with Lentulus' message to Catiline; no doubt the conspirators wanted to seem confident and decisive to their new allies). They also repeated damning claims of Lentulus: that the Sibylline books told of three Cornelii who would rule Rome, his predecessors being Sulla and

Cinna (so much for the pretensions of Catiline); that the current year was the twentieth since the Capitol had burned and Etruscan sooth-sayers proclaimed it stained with bloodshed in civil war. Volturcius did better than securing a pardon: he was given an official monetary reward, along with the Allobrogian envoys. It is highly likely that Volturcius was planted on Lentulus by Cicero, or at least was turned from his revolutionary duties by an offer he could not refuse. The helpful Allobroges had had several hours free to receive their coaching.

When the conspirators were brought before the House they acknowledged their seals on the letters. Gabinius also admitted complicity. The letters were read out and the Senate invited to pronounce. The Senate was convinced – or, at least, members sympa-thetic to Cicero's cause now had a basis for action against sedition at Rome.

Senators, confronted by an apparent threat from one of the most powerful Gallic tribes, remembered everything from the Gauls' sack of Rome at the beginning of the fourth century BC to the invasions of the Celtic Cimbri and Teutones in the last decade of the second. In the Allobroges Cicero found the potent incentive for the Senate to repress sedition with the utmost severity; the Gauls were still a terror 130 years after the conspiracy of Catiline, when the Capitol burned during the Civil Wars after the death of Nero. Senators were invited to interpret the content of the letters as a betrayal of the Republic, and that offence had always been punished by death in one form or another. The legend of Tarpeia offered the prototype. Any senators who may still have felt doubts about the exact purport of the letters could not demur against the majority opinion. The letters were probably ambiguous, offering the Allobroges support in relieving their problems if they helped their new patrons improve the government at Rome and the calibre of Roman magistrates; that very ambiguity bespoke guilt.

The Catilinarian Conspiracy of 63

At this stage, 3 December, the Senate voted that Lentulus Sura should resign his office and that all five conspirators (including M. Caeparius of Tarracina, who had been captured in flight outside the city) should be consigned to the care of senators. Cleverly the consul included Crassus and the praetor designate Caesar among the custodians. They were given Gabinius and Statilius respectively, committing them to the reputable side and winning them a modicum of credit with the optimates. Lentulus was put into the charge of the aedile P. Lentulus Spinther, member of another branch of the Cornelii, and Cethegus and Caeparius of Q. Cornificius, candidate for the consulship of 63, and Cn. Terentius, praetor designate. Cassius remained to be arrested and four lesser figures were also to be detained: P. Furius of Faesulae, M. Annius Chilo, and the freedman Umbrenus.

The Senate voted a thanksgiving for Cicero's having delivered Rome from fire, its citizens from murder, and Italy from war. The mention of fire was enough to win over the plebs, who were cruelly vulnerable to it. Like the threat of Gauls (not that the Allobroges could have had any intention of attacking Rome itself) it guaranteed the success of Cicero's third 'Catilinarian' speech, delivered before them on the same busy day, 3 December.

Other interpretations of this episode of the letters seem too far-fetched to accept. If they were Ciceronian forgeries, planted on the ambassadors, why did the conspirators acknowledge their seals in front of the Senate? They might have been tortured or cajoled by false promises into doing it. That is implausible. But we hear of no attempt on their part or on that of their friends to discredit the evidence. In particular there is the difficulty of the seals; they must have been found in the conspirators' houses in Rome, or used while they were on their fingers during the hours they were imprisoned. All this they allowed to pass in silence, with no appeal to sympathetic or even conniving senators. Crassus apparently absented himself from

78 Catiline

the extempore meeting (he is not named) and we may well ask how well attended it was. Yet Julius Caesar, now Pontifex Maximus and designated to a praetorship of 62, was present and ready to brave the high place in the speaking order that went with his position. There is no sign of an appeal to him, although he had to be careful in the face of senatorial and equestrian opinion.

A senatorial free-for-all

On the following day, 4 December, a dissident who had been making his way to Catiline and who had been arrested en route, so it was said, was brought into the Senate and said that he would give information in return for a pardon. This was L. Tarquinius, whose name neatly attested Etruscan origins: the old kings of Rome had been Tarquins. The first part of his evidence, which corroborated that of Volturcius on the commonplace items (arson, slaughter of respectable citizens, route of the rebels), was well received. But Tarquinius went on to something more contentious: he claimed that he had been sent by Crassus to encourage Catiline; he should not be alarmed by the arrests but advance more quickly on Rome and save the conspirators. This revelation provoked three responses – effectively the same: from those who could not believe it of a man in Crassus' position (the message itself seems unnecessary and even ridiculous); from those who believed in it but thought that Crassus was a man in all circumstances to be placated, not provoked; then there were Crassus' debtors. The charge was cried down and an enquiry demanded. Cicero in a full Senate had the testimony declared false and the witness sent into custody until he revealed his backer. Of the two main suspects for this role, one was P. Autronius, who was supposed to count on protection for himself and the others if he could involve Crassus. The other was Cicero himself, with the idea of paralyzing Crassus and preventing

The Catilinarian Conspiracy of 63　　　79

him from (in Sallust's words) 'taking up the cause of the wicked' in his usual style. Crassus was known for defending clients whose cases had been refused by other distinguished speakers. Sallust claims that he actually heard Crassus complaining of Cicero as the author of the slander, and that, along with the anonymous letters, explains Crassus' animosity to Cicero in the fifties. Certainly Cicero published a work implicating Crassus, after the latter's death. But in 63 Cicero had real, vulnerable targets. Both Crassus and Caesar were too big, too clever, and in Crassus' case too rich to implicate. They had to be neutralized.

Other attempts were made by optimate politicians to bring down opponents at this opportune moment. Sallust names Q. Catulus and C. Piso (consul 67), who did their best with money and political clout to get Cicero to implicate Caesar, using the Allobroges or some other informer, but failed. Catulus was the senior optimate consular who had been defeated by Caesar in the election for the post of Pontifex Maximus. Piso's grudge arose from his having been trounced by Caesar in a trial for misgovernment in which Caesar scored points by demanding justice for Cisalpine Gaul. His enemies were successful at least in egging on a gang of young equestrians, Cicero's bodyguard, to threaten Caesar as he left the Senate.

'Trial' and execution of the conspirators

Meanwhile the adherents of Lentulus, his freedmen and some of his clients, were trying to organize a rescue party from workmen, slaves and hired gang-leaders. Cornelius Cethegus was making his own attempts to free himself, sending messages to his slaves and freedmen, specially chosen and trained; they should marshal themselves, take up arms, and force their way in to him. In this conspiracy it was every man for himself. And the two Cornelii had rich resources of manpower.

80 Catiline

We possess contemporary evidence for the transactions in the Senate on 5 December 63 that led to the execution of the five conspirators; Cicero's speech, duly edited, is supplemented by the later accounts of Sallust, Cassius Dio, Plutarch (in four different works) and Appian. But the course of events and order of speakers is still not clear. It has even been suggested that there were two debates, on successive days, but it is hard to believe that Cicero would have allowed discussion of the proposed sentences to drag out; he wanted crisp action. It was on 5 December that the punishment was decided and carried out. After Cicero's introductory speech, and the deployment of the evidence, the Senate proceeded in due order to give its recommendations. The consul designate, D. Junius Silanus and his colleague, L. Murena came first and firmly expressed the opinion that the accused deserved death, both the five already in custody and L. Cassius, P. Furius, P. Umbrenus and Q. Annius (all associated with the Allobroges). Silanus was followed by former consuls in order of seniority, without dissent. It was soon Caesar's turn as praetor designate. His argument, according to Sallust, was that, appalling as the conspirators' offence was, they should not be executed but permanently confined in one or other Italian town (or, according to Plutarch, until the entire conspiracy was put down). Caesar would not dare to minimize the offence – far from it – but had to take it as manifest, and that makes Plutarch's idea that he called the death penalty 'unjust' extremely unlikely. Imprisonment was the best he could do, and it was of some help to the men, because his offering of a third possibility – between letting them off (impossible in the face of conservative opinion) and killing them – tacitly drew attention to the fact that they had not had a trial in any court established by statute, which would have had a fixed penalty, and that summarily executing them put the Senate in the wrong: Roman citizens enjoyed legal protection from physical violence. The trouble that followed the lynching of the Gracchi and of Saturninus showed

The Catilinarian Conspiracy of 63

what might happen if due process was not followed. Caesar had given a vivid reminder of that earlier in the year when he had C. Rabirius on trial. Now his powerful speech gave pause to senators who followed. Another speaker, Tiberius Claudius Nero, an ex-praetor, brought forward a similar motion, one even safer from a legal point of view. He proposed that the guilty men be kept in custody until the rising was over and orderly trials under statute law could be held.

It looked now as if the five conspirators were to escape with their lives, even though their careers were over and their property would be confiscated, for D. Silanus withdrew his original proposal for the death penalty (he had been misunderstood, he said). This was an alarm signal for Cicero: insurrections in Italy would fail only if the participants heard that their potential allies had been wiped out. It was vital that the men should not survive anywhere, especially in Italian towns, to become a focus for rescue attempts and insurrections. Cicero may now have intervened again (with his 'fourth Catilinarian'). But it was Q. Catulus, who had already spoken amongst the ex-consulars, and M. Porcius Cato, tribune designate, who came to his rescue. Sallust sets Cato's speech against Caesar's showing his admiration for the divergent qualities of the two men: conciliation and flexibility on the part of Caesar, stern and inflexible integrity on Cato's. Modelling himself on his great ancestor the Censor, Cato was an extreme optimate for whom political life without the Republic as he knew it was unthinkable. Seventeen years later he proved that when he killed himself at Utica in Africa on being defeated by Caesar's forces in the Civil War. Now he spoke out: there could be no compromise. Caesar was devising an unheard-of punishment and endangering the state. Perpetual imprisonment, he claimed, was a worse punishment than death, which was quick. The remaining speakers, including all the ex-consuls according to Sallust, rallied to Cato. Caesar's objection to the confiscation of their property, which ruined the prospects of their children, received no help from the tribunes and it was rejected.

82 *Catiline*

Cicero's view won the day, and he conducted the conspirators to the Tullianum, beginning with Lentulus, who came down from his place of detention on the Palatine along the Sacred Way to the cells on the Capitoline Hill. They were let down into the execution chamber and strangled. Cicero came out and announced their fate to the waiting people: 'Their life is over.'

The dispersal of the crowd may have been sullen, but Cicero had his 12 lictors and unofficial attendants to protect him. He had destroyed the conspiracy at Rome, and could sleep quietly that night. The insurrections in Italy, especially that in Etruria, still remained and would have to be dealt with by force. The consul's soldiering days went back to Asculum; he was not a soldier and could not contain a widespread emergency that needed flexibility of strategy and tactics for dealing with irregulars organized by an experienced veteran officer and led by an ex-praetor with distinguished military service to his credit.

Cicero could call on two main forces: one was that of Q. Caecilius Metellus, a seasoned army waiting for its commander to triumph; the other could be recruited at once and led by Cicero's colleague in the consulship, M. Antonius. Antonius was disreputable, suspect to the conservatives, sympathetic to the conspirators, and in Cassius Dio's account had actually taken the oath to Catiline. But he had long since been promised his reward, Macedonia. Catiline was now dodging about, moving sometimes towards Rome, sometimes towards Cisalpine Gaul. He hoped to pick up more supporters, especially if the men in Rome had had any success. He still resolutely avoided the help of slaves. Only at the very end is there a hint that he gave way.

Meanwhile, in Rome, Cicero was still providing moral leadership. Towards the end of the year, in Plutarch's account, he providentially received a sign of favour from the gods. The women-only festival of the Bona Dea was held in his house, as that of the most senior magistrate, but as a male he had to spend the night away. His wife Terentia, who was conducting the rites, told him of a flame that burst out from an altar in the house. Cicero's brother Quintus and his friend and supporter, the savant P. Nigidius Figulus arrived (presumably after the ceremonies were over) to witness the phenomenon and give it the solidity of masculine and senatorial backing. It was a sign of favour from heaven and, when reported in the Senate and to the Roman priesthood, stood Cicero in good stead.

The battle of Pistoria and the death of Catiline

The decisive military clash took place in early January 62 near Pistoria (Pistoia), about 30 kilometres north-west of Florence. News of the executions had shaken Catiline's followers, and the less determined, chancers or opportunists, slipped away; but Catiline led the core, 3,000 men according to Dio, 6,000 on the reckoning of Diodorus, into territory from which they could, if it came to it, make their way into Gaul on the other side of the Alps. Catiline's movements in this campaign have been elucidated by G. V. Sumner. They show him, even at a distance from Rome and in the last days of his life, making politicians dance. Encamped near Faesulae, he knew that the consul Antonius was approaching from the south. Catiline withdrew his troops into the hills, poised to return if a success at Rome brought him new recruits. When news of the catastrophe at Rome reached him he began to lead them towards Pistoria by devious routes; that would eventually give him access to the territory of the Allobroges, who were not all free from suspicion.

But the praetor Q. Metellus Celer, whose three legions were garrisoning Picenum to the east, the Ager Gallicus, and Cisalpina, with the aid of C. Murena, brother of the new consul, discovered the plan from captured stragglers and occupied the routes that led from the mountains, while the presence of Antonius in the west probably forced Catiline to take the roundabout and rough route that Sallust specifies, and which took him about nine days down the River Renus to be within striking distance of Bononia (Bologna) on what Sumner calculates to be 25 December. Catiline had to turn back across the Apennines and instead face the advancing Antonius, who by early January was being urged on by the quaestor P. Sestius and his reinforcements. Catiline was near Pistoria in the first days of January.

The force was trapped and would have to fight its way out, whether towards Gaul or – hardly likely now – against Rome. On the day of the battle Antonius was unable to take part in person because of a foot complaint, presumably gout. He left the work, and the ill repute it brought, to his legate, the experienced military man and ex-praetor M. Petreius, who was eventually to take up arms again on the side of Pompey against Caesar, committing suicide at the end. Gout did not prevent Antonius from sending Catiline's head to Rome and from being acclaimed *imperator*, according to Dio, although the numbers of enemy slain did not meet the requirement for a Triumph (6,000) – and these dead were overwhelmingly Roman citizens. (Three thousand is the lowest estimate, from Dio; 6,000 from Diodorus and Appian's 10,000 are clearly too many.) On the other hand, we hear that Antonius felt so badly about his role that he made his troops wipe their weapons clean before they re-entered camp.

In a hard-fought battle Catiline fought as hard as any, occupying the centre with the eagle that Marius was said to have deployed in his army in the war against the Cimbri. Like many Roman villains, Catiline is portrayed as a man with the virtues of his class, especially *virtus* itself – manliness, courage. When he knew he had lost his lieutenants and saw his troops in defeat he threw himself into the thick of the enemy; his body was said to have been found next day transfixed with wounds on the front. In a familiar trope of battle stories, he was still breathing – and his face still looking as ferocious as it had in life.

The Catilinarian Conspiracy of 63   85

Sallust pays tribute to the resolution shown on both sides. All that remained was to mop up resistance from irregulars in other areas. The commitment of officers was not to be questioned: the praetors Q. Cicero (Marcus' brother) tackled the Bruttii, M. Bibulus the Paeligni. The job was still going on in 60, when C. Octavius distinguished himself by defeating remnants in southern Italy. The origins of the rising in Etruria and elsewhere and the planned takeover of Rome were distinct, though they had factors in common: the debt of the participants. One was almost wholly economic, the other concerned with as well with status (*dignitas*). It does not do to divorce them entirely, however. When radical politicians stood for and reached office, as radical tribunes did in mid-64, and others were standing for praetorship and consulship, urban and rural voters alike will have flocked to support them and made themselves known to them, promising their support in return for economic, political and social reform. It may not be quite accurate to claim that the risings in Italy would have taken place regardless of Catiline: for all the disappointment of urban and rural masses, they might not have risen if they had had no hope of being led by a blue-blooded politician.

6

The Aftermath of Catiline: Cicero's Struggle to Survive

A shortlived triumph

At Rome Cicero had achieved his aim and carried out his promise to the optimates to wipe out revolution and even reform wherever it appeared. During the year the people had had their hopes of land distribution dashed; their champions were defeated, five were already dead. At the end of the year Cato, tribune of the plebs since 10 December, made a conciliatory and necessary gesture of increasing the number of citizens eligible for the dole of free grain at Rome. He had seen the mob milling around the Senate House. Although Cato publicly dubbed him 'Father of the Fatherland' and in the House seconded a motion put forward by Q. Catulus for the conferment of the title, Cicero knew that he would get no more thanks for saving their constitution from the rest of the optimates; they grudged this new man his consulship just as much and his success all the more.

From his youth Cicero had seen political fortunes swaying from one side to the other, from Sulla to the Marians and back. There would be a backlash. Not only would the relatives, friends, dependants and secret sympathizers of Catiline detest him. Principled politicians – jurisconsults, for example, who held to the rule of law – found his methods unacceptable, in particular his execution of five Roman citizens, one of them a praetor, without due process. The Lex Sempronia that Gaius Gracchus had passed in 123 BC in a vain attempt to prevent judicial murders ordered by the Senate, such as followed his brother's death in 133, forbade anyone's 'judicial removal' and the pronouncing of a verdict on any Roman citizen 'without the instruction of the Roman People'. It was still on the statute book. There was no way back for Cicero: the optimates had not hired him for the one year, they had bought him outright.

Cato and his fellow tribunes of the plebs had been elected under the presidency of one of the radical college that had put forward the Rullan Bill. At the end of December Cicero left office. He had to go to the Capitol as his predecessors had done and take an oath that his actions had been in the interests of the state. Two new tribunes, Q. Metellus Nepos and L. Calpurnius Bestia, stepped in, along with the praetor Caesar, and prevented him from doing it. Nepos denounced Cicero and by implication the Senate as a body for condemning citizens to death without the consent of the people. He could expect trouble from them. Cicero succeeded in taking an oath, reworded: he had saved the Republic. But he needed strong allies, and there was one who might soon be glad of the help of an authoritative consular with supreme oratorical gifts. Cicero wrote to Pompey in the east describing his own achievements and congratulating Pompey on his, a letter whose contents somehow became widely known.

Cicero and Pompey

In 63 Pompey completed his work in the east. Mithridates VI Eupator had also completed his life by ending it himself. News of that reached Rome in the summer, and Cicero ordered a ten-day Thanksgiving in Pompey's honour. Now, after mopping up, Pompey would bring his troops back to Italy and wait outside Rome with any he had not discharged until he was granted a Triumph by the Senate. He had reported all his achievements and the arrangements he had made for

The Aftermath of Catiline: Cicero's Struggle to Survive

the rich new provinces he had annexed, Syria and Pontus-Bithynia, the foundation of cities, and the disposition of client kings. All these people were indeed dependent upon him for their status and on his success in getting his acts ratified by the Senate. In particular the troops wanted their rewards, the grant of plots of land for their retirement. If he failed to secure them his prestige would fade. No wonder one of the new tribunes, Nepos, was motivated, according to the Bobbio Scholiast on Cicero's speech for Sestius, to propose amid violent scenes that Pompey should be elected in absence to a consulship and that he should be appointed to mop up the Catilinarians and their followers, just as he had helped mop up those of Spartacus. In the account of G. V. Sumner, he was trying to secure the command before Catiline was annihilated by forces on the spot, some under the command of Nepos' brother Celer. Indeed he brought forward his proposal to one day before the legitimate day (three market days after promulgation). He enjoyed the support of Caesar, and controlled the Forum with gladiators, but his colleagues Cato and Q. Minucius led the optimates in violent scenes against his proposals, and they may never have come to the vote. The bill favouring Pompey could offer only mopping-up operations. All the same, it was fought for, even to another passing of the 'ultimate decree', according to Dio. Cicero's position was strengthened by a defensive resolution of the Senate to the effect that all who had acted against the conspiracy were to be immune from prosecution, and anyone who brought a charge against them was to be considered an enemy of the Roman People. Fine words. But Nepos left Italy for Pompey, now on Rhodes, while Caesar, censured by the House and suspended from office, found it prudent to stay within doors for a month. That did not stop him trying to have Q. Catulus discharged from his task of restoring the ruined Capitol, querying his accounts, and attempting to have the task transferred to Pompey.

Pompey replied to Cicero's report. We do not have his letter, which came along with his official dispatch to the Senate, but only Cicero's

April response to it, a remarkable and illuminating text. Cicero thanked Pompey for the letter and assured him that the dispatch had shattered the hopes of men who had once been Pompey's 'enemies in the field' but were his new-found 'friends' – that is, the popular politicians Pompey had crushed for Sulla but who were now pinning their hopes of change on him. Cicero regretted that Pompey's letter had not been warmer or shown Cicero more esteem. He went on to claim something near parity of achievement and to ask Pompey, the latter-day P. Cornelius Scipio Africanus Aemilianus, the conqueror of Carthage, to regard him, not as an equal, but at least as a latter-day and lesser C. Laelius – the friend of Scipio and the statesman who had withdrawn an agrarian bill and won the title 'Sapiens', 'the Wise'. He was known for his steadfast devotion to Scipio and for his authority as an adviser. This then is the status that Cicero is after, that of being a guide in civil and political life to the great military man. The question is what earned Cicero's right to a similar position in relation to Pompey, and the tacit and shocking answer is that he had done better: he had outwitted him. That was the reason for Pompey's coolness. In Latin three words told it all: '*cedant arma togae*' ('Let weapons give way to civil dress'). No wonder some 'unprincipled' men thought that there would be bad blood between Cicero and Pompey over the affair.

When Cicero undertook to influential optimates, his potential and reluctant electoral supporters, that he would deal decisively with unrest during his consulship, it was not only with Catiline or Manlius or the masses at Rome and elsewhere in mind. It was the chaos that uprisings anywhere in Italy would cause, giving Pompey his chance to return with his army, sort matters out, as he had done with Lepidus in 78 and Spartacus in 71, and make unacceptable political demands for the future. Cicero had undertaken that if Pompey should return in 63 he would not find a consul ready to pass any measure to gratify the conqueror and enhance his power this time, not perhaps with a command in Spain or a consulship, perhaps with the Dictatorship

The Aftermath of Catiline: Cicero's Struggle to Survive   91

that the seriousness of the situation demanded. Without going that far – that was the office that Pompey failed to obtain even in a year of acute domestic crisis, 52, winning the consulship without a colleague instead – we would be justified in thinking of a second consulship, with ratification of his acts the least of his other demands. This was the ploy that Metellus Nepos did attempt, unsuccessfully, at the beginning of 62, when Catiline and his forces were still in the field. Confronted by optimate hostility, all that Nepos could achieve was to flee Rome, ostentatiously, and return to Pompey.

It happened that two of the men who opposed the immediate execution of the conspirators at Rome were connected with Pompey: Caesar, who had supported the bill giving Pompey the command against the pirates in 67, and Ti. Claudius Nero, who had been Pompey's legate during the pirate war. They might have regarded with complacency the survival of the conspirators in light imprisonment that gave hope of releasing them. Cicero would have none of that. The optimates too had seen Pompey's father's technique in the Civil War of 88, Pompey's own in 77 and 71. This gave Cicero an overriding, perhaps unexpressed commission, and he fully understood it. Cicero had to jettison a friend and act against him on behalf of men who hated Pompey and despised Cicero. What reward had he won? Only an old prize, the consulship itself and after it the status of a consular. Along with them had come enormous risks, assassination or a legal assault.

Catiline and Pompey

We have just seen Cicero in correspondence with Pompey in the east. He cannot have been Pompey's only correspondent and informant. The question has to be asked, whether Catiline had also been one of their number. For as far as any political arrangements he might make, whether as consul, legitimately elected or usurping, he would have to take account of Pompey's imminent return. For him as well as for the optimates Pompey was the great unknown quantity. I suggest that Catiline was in correspondence with Pompey at least from the moment he returned from governing Africa, and that when he promised political reform in the run-up to the consular elections of 63, he did so with the acquiescence of Pompey, and on the understanding that, if elected, he would do all that was necessary to satisfy Pompey's needs on his return, despite all that enemies in the Senate could do. When Catiline's final canvass failed he will have informed Pompey of this too. Whatever he had planned at this stage, there can be no doubt of his keeping his options open as far as Pompey was concerned. The letter would have to be carefully drafted. Indignation at the tactics of the optimates carried through by Cicero, which was no doubt shared by Pompey, would have justified Catiline in undertaking to defend his status – the factor that in 49 justified Julius Caesar in crossing the River Rubicon and beginning civil war. Catiline would not have been specific about the methods he intended to use, nor would Pompey have replied with any phrase that would have discouraged him. Whatever means Catiline used to defend his status were satisfactory to Pompey; he would return to find either a compliant consul or a situation in which he would once again be required by a helpless Senate to restore order. He could not lose.

With this scenario, timing was everything for Catiline. He needed the rebellion to break out just as Pompey set sail for Brundisium and to reach its peak when he arrived, preferably with Rome in the hands of the rebels and ready to greet the returning hero, who would fulfil their demands as well as his own needs and those of his troops. Catiline would be a loyal ally, rewarded with his long-sought consulship and a provincial command to follow. What must not happen was that the Italian rebellions should go off prematurely, allowing the forces of conservatism to quash them before they could be useful to Pompey. But the Italians could not be held back, and

The Aftermath of Catiline: Cicero's Struggle to Survive   93

Catiline had to join them. The Allobroges could have been a bonus, keeping Roman commanders away from the core of the rebellion in central and northern Italy.

The question immediately arises, how quickly letters could pass between Rome and Pompey's headquarters, and back again. In early December 63, when Cicero wrote him his boastful report, Pompey was probably wintering at Amisus (Samsun) on the coast of Pontus, and Cicero had his chilling reply before April. That particular exchange took up to four months; correspondence that resulted from Catiline's final rejection in July should have taken less time, even to Jerusalem. But the known times for messages, even using the Augustan public horse, are still too varied to allow us to guess how long Catiline's carriers would have taken over different routes and changing seasons.

There is nothing of any connivance between Catiline and Pompey in the sources; on the contrary, Sallust merely states that when Catiline took his first active steps towards revolution, at the beginning of June, 64 BC (an anachronism, but that is irrelevant for the present issue), it was an encouragement to him that 'Pompey was carrying on a war at the ends of the earth'. But nothing should be expected; the correspondence would be secret, nothing came of it, thanks to Cicero's bravery, and nothing would have been said of it in public at the time: 'Talk of the Devil, and he's sure to appear'. This is the place for a final look at the canard about Crassus' involvement with Catiline's conspiracy. Nothing could be further from the truth. Crassus had seen Pompey returning to Italy in force nearly a decade before, when he was dealing with Spartacus and had to share the glory of his success with Pompey. In 63 he was a civilian with no prospect of a command. Plutarch tells how, when Pompey was returning to Rome in 62, Crassus fled, taking his treasure chests with him. It was a strange flight, along the Via Egnatia through northern Greece and making for Asia Minor, close to the route that Pompey

94 *Catiline*

would have followed in reverse, when he brought his army back to Italy, by way of Dyrrhachium (Durrës) and Brundisium (Brindisi). They could have met for a frank discussion, notably about the strong position of common opponents among the optimates, after the suppression of Catiline's conspiracy. No doubt Cicero's achievements were given due consideration. Crassus then proceeded on his way to the provinces of Pontus-Bithynia and Asia, where he set up fresh financial arrangements for the cities there, lending money for their resurgence in the new era of peace and cushioning their relations with the tax-gatherers – though these Asian transactions were to bring Crassus new problems.

Pompey must reach Italy in 62 at latest, so Cicero knew that the insurrections had to be dealt with speedily, with no survivors lingering in municipal detention and no substantial rebel army left standing. If necessary, he must provoke dissidents into action, work he had begun when he prevented Catiline's election, and this was what he went on to do between the election and his first Catilinarian speech. There was only a narrow window of opportunity: conspiracy was hardly a credible charge when Catiline was still a candidate for the consulship and his followers still entertained hopes of change by legal means. He had to act after the elections, though it would be speculation to suppose that he sent *agents provocateurs* among the dispossessed in Rome, even more fanciful to think of them operating in Italy. He took a risk in goading Catiline; he might after all have taken the road for Massilia.

Cicero's breach of statute law

Cicero also took a potentially fatal risk in executing the five conspirators. He had no legal basis for it at all, and it was only the threat of lynching by an angry elite or by hired thugs at the doors to the Senate

The Aftermath of Catiline: Cicero's Struggle to Survive   95

that kept Caesar from saying so. The conspirators were safely in custody and should have been protected from death by C. Gracchus' famous law. It was irrelevant that the conspirators were 'tried' in the Senate (two days' hearing at most). There was no 'instruction from the people', that is, no court established by duly enacted statute and staffed at this period by senators, equestrians, and members of a class less than theirs. The main reason for Cicero's drastic action, apart from the fact that he thought that senators were sensitive to anti-senatorial plots and afterwards would be forced as a body to back him, was that setting up the jury court took time: the praetor in charge of the court had to be approached, a day for the hearing appointed, the jurymen (sometimes more than 100) appointed and scrutinized (all of which gave time for the accused to flee into exile). After that, prosecution and defence were allocated fixed periods of time for their arguments and evidence; a trial might last several days. Accused men often fled even in the course of a trial if was going against them: so Verres.

Under the Principate men and women were regularly tried in the Senate, and sometimes executed. One has only to read a few pages of Tacitus' *Annals* to realize this. This was because it was to the advantage of the emperor to have cases heard in a body he could control by controlling the future careers of the 'jurymen'. In a pernicious move towards autocracy, Augustus, once firmly in power from 19 BC onwards, regularly put cases of political importance to the Senate, depriving the courts of their prerogative. The case of Catiline's fellow conspirators ironically became a model.

It has been brought on in favour of Cicero's legal and political position that the so-called 'Ultimate Decree' had been passed in October, when news reached Rome of the rising in Etruria. The phrase is shorthand for a decree passed by the Senate enjoining the consuls, praetors, and other magistrates 'to ensure that the state came to no harm', and it is that of Sallust in his account of the events of

63; sources present the decree in variant wordings. It had been used first in the optimate struggle against Gaius Gracchus in 121, after he failed to win a third successive tribunate. Violence had developed into a riot. Gaius and his closest associates took refuge on the traditionally plebeian Aventine Hill, were sought out and massacred. The consul responsible, L. Opimius, had then taken advantage of the decree to shelter behind the Senate's authority – for that was all the decree provided, a promise of political protection if illegal action was challenged. Opimius was indeed challenged, but he was acquitted. Fear of Gracchan violence was still rife, and money was potent too. Only in the next period of popular activity was Opimius punished, and then merely for robbing his provincial subjects. The second time the decree was deployed also led to later legal wrangles; this was in 100 BC when the consul Marius and his colleagues (the serving praetor Servilius Glaucia, Saturninus' ally, was excluded from the action) were instructed to protect the state from the activities of Saturninus. The violence of 100 led to another flurry of prosecutions, ending in the attack on Rabirius. Caesar was trying to limit the use of the decree for the elimination of Roman citizens, and offering a warning to Cicero, which he chose not to hear. It may well be asked why the Senate continued to use the decree at all. The answer is that that was the only resource they had, since as a body they had no executive power. They had only an advisory capacity. They had seen from previous crises that it was not the Senate as a whole that suffered from the consequences of its use, only the magistrates and their associates who carried out the wishes of the House. The majority of the Senate present in December 63 believed that there was at least one conspiracy in which the five men before them had been involved, and considered it serious enough (given the rising in Italy and the expected arrival of Pompey) to deal with instantly by a method that was outside the law but would not bring them into danger.

Cicero's self-advertisement

Cicero, who had already given up Macedonia to M. Antonius, did not take up a province and leave Rome to its fate under the consuls of 62. Such a retreat would have delivered a blow to the continuous authority of senatorial government. He was in a sense the hero of the hour, and had he removed himself, even on official business, he would lose credit and the current officials would lose courage. Besides, the defeat of Catiline's forces did not come until January 62. There was still danger. After that, Cicero must prepare what defences he could. Publicity for the hero was one, however ineffective. Cicero could claim that he was the target of assassins, the supporters of Catiline, years after the rebel's death and when he was himself in exile in Macedonia. In speeches and letters Cicero did not cease to refer to his saving of the state, to such an extent that he has become a subject of mockery not only among his contemporaries but to modern students who fail to understand the purpose of the blast. By contrast Caesar, under threat from his political enemies in the fifties and forties, composed self-glorifying *Gallic* and *Civil Wars*, but has avoided ridicule: those volumes had substance.

The trial of P. Sulla

In 62 Cicero had to undertake another defence, reverting, as he had done for Murena, to an earlier form of activity. His client was P. Sulla, the man who had lost the consulship in 66 when he was convicted of electoral bribery. Now, probably between May and October, he was charged like others already familiar – Autronius, Vargunteius, Servius Sulla and his sibling, another P. Sulla, M. Laeca – under the statute on violence The accuser was a man who had turned state's evidence,

L. Vettius, for complicity in the Catilinarian conspiracy and, in Sulla's case, involvement in the disturbances of 66–65, the 'first Catilinarian conspiracy'. Vettius had clearly been privy to Catiline's plans. He happened to be known to him from long ago, as yet another member of Pompeius Strabo's advisory board; like Catiline, he had done well from Sulla's confiscations.

Cicero's authoritative evidence in these cases, ensuring automatic conviction, only added to his unpopularity; Nepos' crack, reported by Plutarch, that Cicero's evidence had assured more executions than his eloquence had secured acquittals, would hit a mark. An even more vitriolic attack is to be found in the anonymous (perhaps Augustan) *Invective against Cicero*: he had made himself rich from the blood and suffering of his fellow-citizens. For, the story runs, Cicero had had men into his house and he and his wife Terentia had forced them to disgorge money under threat of a prosecution backed with his expertise on the Catilinarian conspiracy. As to the charge that Sulla had been involved with Catiline, Sulla and Autronius had planned a massacre at the election of 63, and Sulla had bought gladiators (as any ambitious politician might, to enhance his prestige with the populace). He was linked by the prosecution not only with dissidents in Pompeii, but with the Allobroges, and evidence on that point had been falsified by Cicero as soon as it had been presented to the Senate. Whether Sulla was involved with the Catilinarians remains uncertain. Certainly he intervened in politics at Pompeii – but Pompeii did not rise. He was probably gathering support to use either for Catiline or against him; as to the gladiators, they were for his cousin Faustus' games, so it emerged. And the conspirator Cassius had said that he 'did not know' whether Sulla was with them. It was not only Cicero but Q. Hortensius and other optimates who stood up for Sulla in 62.

There was now no longer any excuse for a kangaroo court; due process was expected. Not surprisingly P. Sulla's prosecutor was again

The Aftermath of Catiline: Cicero's Struggle to Survive 99

the son of Torquatus, consul in 65, aided by a C. Cornelius, son of a man already condemned, who was keen to refurbish the reputation of his family. In one sense the trial was a blessing for Cicero, in that it helped to keep Catiline and his crimes before the eyes of the public and showed that he was no bigot of the Senator McCarthy type, but it was also an embarrassment, and he might not have undertaken Sulla's case but for the political and monetary debts he owed his client: in the course of the prosecution, Sulla lent Cicero two million HS, more than half the cost of his new house on the Palatine. Cicero wryly wrote to a friend that he was so much in debt that he would willingly join a conspiracy, if someone would take him on; but apart from hating the man who had been the nemesis of a conspiracy, his ruined opponents would not believe that one who had saved the money-lenders from attack would not be flush.

For Sulla it was a coup to retain Cicero, the high authority on the movement. The charge extended to Sulla's activities as a member of the 'conspiracy' of 66–65. Cicero was just as much an expert on that, and that was one source of embarrassment in defending Sulla. Had he not developed it in his election speech of 64, *In toga candida*, from its original form of a conspiracy on the part of Sulla and his partner Autronius into the first *Catilinarian* conspiracy? Now, the astute prosecutor of Sulla thought, Cicero could be pinned down to his own fiction. But Cicero was not so easy to pin down. He deployed his 'expertise' on matters Catilinarian to exonerate Sulla. He even went so far as to claim that the targets of the first 'conspiracy', Torquatus, the father of Sulla's prosecutor, had 'indicated' that he knew nothing of any such plot. Young Torquatus was savage; not only did he suggest that Cicero alone was responsible for the deaths of Lentulus and the others, he invoked Cicero as an expert on the conspiracy of 66–65, and Cicero was forced into a desperate reply: at that time he was not yet versed in politics and was not privy to the counsels of Torquatus' father. That will have raised a titter, coming from the praetor of 66. But it was more than a feeble joke if the real plot had been constructed by the Torquati against their enemy Sulla – and that surely was what Cicero now implied that the 'counsels' of Torquatus were. Cicero's defence of Sulla was to spirit him out of the 'conspiracy' of 66–65 and replace him with Catiline, safely dead and available for any villainy; Catiline, Piso, Vargunteius and Autronius were accepted villains who needed no help from Sulla.

P. Clodius and the Bona Dea celebrations of 62

The trial of Sulla was an insignificant aftershock to the conspiracy, compared with the convulsions of a trial that took place the following year, which had violent repercussions on the lives of all the leading politicians of the day – that is, the prosecution in May of P. Clodius Pulcher on a charge of having violated the rites of the Bona Dea. In December 62 the chief celebrant had been Pompeia, the wife of the Pontifex Maximus Caesar. The charge was that Clodius, disguised as a woman lute-player, and intent on pursuing a love affair, entered the house while the rites were being carried on. Infringement was a serious matter, for the rite involved Rome's relations with the gods and so the security of the Roman People.

Clodius was member of one of Rome's most ancient, aristocratic and allegedly arrogant houses, that of the Claudii, who had migrated to Rome from the Sabine territory early in its history and played a prominent part in politics ever since, sometimes with distinction, sometimes to its disgrace. Clodius was the son of Appius Claudius Pulcher, a leading light of the Sullan restoration, first to hold the consulship after Sulla had inaugurated it in 80. Clodius, like his sister, the notorious muse of the poet Catullus, preferred to spell his name in the Sabine way (for so it would be pronounced in that area), which had plebeian connotations.

The Aftermath of Catiline: Cicero's Struggle to Survive   101

One story is that he was trapped and recognized by the maidservants of Aurelia, Caesar's mother, was pushed out of the house and made off. In Cicero's version he was helped to escape by a female slave. In any case he invoked an alibi: he had been at Interamna (Terni, 104 kilometres north of Rome) on the day of the festival. It was his word against the women's. The conservative core of the Senate under L. Lucullus was determined to see Clodius convicted of sacrilege. Lucullus had been conducting the war against Mithridates VI when Clodius egged his troops on to mutiny; besides, there was the collateral damage that could be done to Caesar. The claim that Clodius was committing incest with his sister, Lucullus' wife, was a sensationalist optional extra. Clodius' alibi was broken by none other than Cicero, who testified, despite a demonstration against him, that he had seen Clodius at Rome on the day of the celebration. Nonetheless, the jury acquitted Clodius by 31 to 25, with a majority of the jurors spoiling their voting tablets – and so avoiding offence to people and nobility, says Plutarch. It was a result of bribery, Cicero claimed, and he was probably right. Where did the money come from? Crassus is the standard backer of politicians who were against the *status quo*, and one of Cicero's letters has been interpreted as indicating his help. But Pompey contributed vast sums to the State Treasury when he returned from the east; he was far richer than Crassus and it may have been Pompey who paid off the jury at Clodius' trial. The man's activities as a junior officer in Lucullus' army had led indirectly to Pompey's own appointment against Mithridates, and he might prove useful, if not immediately as a current quaestor, then later in his career. If Pompey did spend money on Clodius' future, his investment was unsound. The aristocrat was not to be bought; he proved first unreliable as tribune in 58, then downright hostile to Pompey himself.

Can any sense be read into this grotesque affair? If Clodius did enter the house in disguise, it could have been for a variety of reasons.

First, he did want to pursue an affair, with Caesar's wife Pompeia or another woman. But that might have been better done in a less frequented place; we have to assume that the danger added spice to his game. Alternatively, he may have been intending to damage the reputation of Pompeia, and so to break the influence of the praetor and Pontifex Maximus, Caesar. There is no evidence for enmity between the two. Caesar kept out of the prosecution, but divorced his wife, with the alleged comment that 'Caesar's wife must be above suspicion'. He seems to have preferred being on good terms with Clodius to keeping close to Pompeia's optimate kin (she belonged to a different branch of the Pompeii from that of the general). A third possibility is that Clodius' escapade was just that. It is not plausible, if only because Clodius was within days of entering his quaestorship at the time, and so about 30 years old.

One particular puzzle is Clodius' identification by Aurelia. If we accept her testimony, and assume that she was not mistaken, we have to choose one of the three explanations above. But perhaps she was mistaken, and Clodius was being framed. The Aurelii Cottae belonged to the innermost circle of the oligarchy and held consulships in 75 and 74. The possible damage to her son Caesar was not great. Of Aurelia's relations with her daughter-in-law, we know nothing, except that Aurelia is said to have been constantly with her at the festival. She may have preferred another woman for Caesar.

After his quaestorship Clodius sought to be transferred from his patrician status to the plebeian order, so that he might be elected to the tribunate of the plebs. Clodius, after his trial, was one of those politicians whose advance in the Senate had been blocked and who took up popular causes. Even the Gracchi have been seen in this light. Clodius was known later as 'Felix Catilina' – 'Catiline with better luck'. Revenge and reform, he calculated, would make his career to the consulship and beyond. He calculated correctly up to a point, but died in a brawl in 52, ironically at the hands of one of Pompey's adherents.

The Bona Dea affair and the prosecution of Clodius may be seen as another phase in the scheme of the oligarchy to bring down radicals, including Caesar, the bolder because by December 62 Catiline's cause was lost and there was nothing to fear from Pompey's return. The *popularis* tribune C. Fufius Calenus was largely instrumental in securing Clodius' acquittal; later he was to be found with Caesar in the Civil War, and then again with Mark Antony. If this was the aim of the prosecution, it helps to explain why Cicero had to join in. He had committed himself to the optimates when they were concerned about Catiline and Manlius, and now he had to be consistent. He had nowhere else to go, saw the popular cause reviving – and kept with the grandees.

So Cicero's ambition for the consulship, his annihilation of the Catilinarians, and his consequent involvement in the Bona Dea affair had crippling consequences for him. Worse were to come. To the popular backlash that was inevitable when severe and longstanding grievances remained and men of rank had been illegally killed, there was added the hatred of Clodius.

Pompey's problems and their solution

Pompey's frustration did not end in 62. After landing, he had disbanded his army and entered Rome accompanied only by his personal bodyguard. That was what Cicero's destruction of Catiline forced on him. Not surprisingly, in 61 Cicero's first letter to Atticus mentions the general view that Pompey was 'extremely friendly' to him; by mid-February he felt able to rub Pompey's nose in the felicitous state of the Republic, and in March 60 Pompey was extolling Cicero's achievement in the Senate. After the failure of the tribune Metellus and the Senate's wilful delay in implementing the measures that he needed to maintain his status, he tried to work through consuls. The weak M. Pupius Piso of 61 was Pompey's man; it had been as a compromise with Pompey that the Senate had postponed the elections so that he could arrive in time to stand. So was the Picene L. Afranius, Piso's successor, previously a legate in the east. Neither succeeded in achieving his aims. A person of courage and determination was required. That person was Caesar, who returned from his province of Spain in order to stand for the consulship of 59. He too had problems with senatorial recalcitrance. At the urging of Cato, the House refused to allow Caesar to declare himself a candidate without crossing the sacred boundary of Rome, the Pomerium, and doing that would entail giving up his military authority and forfeiting the Triumph that his successes in Spain had earned him. Caesar gave up the Triumph and made himself available to Pompey as the man who would bring his eastern arrangements legitimacy and, with an agrarian bill, successor to the Rullan Bill of 63, provide for his discharged veterans. No doubt it was Pompey who paid part of his election expenses. But Caesar is usually seen as an ally of Crassus, and it was said to be from him that Caesar had found the money that enabled him to go to his praetorian province at the end of 62. The relationship may not have been one of long standing, but it is easy to accept the idea that Crassus also backed Caesar for the consulship of 59, for Caesar was able to perform a service for him too during that year. The contractors of taxes, excited by Pompey's settlement of the east, had bid high in competition for the contracts available for the well-established and lucrative province of Asia. They were disappointed: Asia Minor, scene of lengthy wars, was short of cash to satisfy tax-men. Through Crassus the latter sought a reduction of the amount they had undertaken to pay to the Treasury. This was naturally resisted in the Senate, whose authority in the Empire depended on its revenues. The argument had been going

The Aftermath of Catiline: Cicero's Struggle to Survive   105

on since 61, and it brought Senate and equestrian order far from the 'concord of the orders' that Cicero tried to establish in 63 in defence of stability and the united supremacy of the propertied classes. It was Caesar as consul in 59 who secured the remission.

These services performed by Caesar for the men who backed his consulship have given rise to the notion of a 'triumvirate', which should properly be a joint magistracy of three men. At most, all that may have been agreed between Pompey and Crassus, if anything, was that neither would thwart the plans of the other. The connexion was not between them but between each of them and Caesar. In 56, when they renewed this agreement, they also agreed on five-year commands abroad for each of them: Caesar to remain in his Gallic province for another five years, Pompey to take Spain, and Crassus the east. That made the arrangement look more like a 'triumvirate', but no triumvirate in the proper sense came into being until 43, when Mark Antony, Marcus Aemilius Lepidus, both aides of the assassinated Dictator Caesar, and his grand-nephew Octavian, the later Emperor Augustus, undertook a joint rule over the entire Empire, to last another five years: they called themselves 'Triumvirs for the establishment of the Constitution'. Crassus was killed campaigning against the Parthians in 53, and the marriage between Pompey and Caesar's daughter Julia had come to an end the year before when she died in childbirth. Pompey's next wife was a Cornelia of the Scipios. He allowed himself to be won over to the cause of the optimates, who were intent now on destroying Caesar. When the struggle came in 49 Pompey could not match Caesar's generalship; he was defeated at Pharsalus in Greece in 48 and assassinated in Egypt by its Ptolemaic ruler.

It had been Cicero's repression of the insurrections in Italy and his extirpation of the conspirators at Rome, then, that led to the straits that Pompey found himself in in 62–60. Instead of submitting to the humiliation intended for him he joined two other ambitious

106 *Catiline*

individuals in taking all the prizes in the political game, making it not worth playing for any politician who meant to keep to the old rules. The Catilinarian conspiracy led to the 'First Triumvirate' and ultimately to the civil war that broke out in 49.

Cicero exiled

Ten years previously Cicero claimed that he had been invited to join the counsels of the three dynasts, and had refused. It was an honourable mistake. If he had had their protection he would have been safe from the attacks of Clodius in 58. Instead he was gloating in July 59 over the discomfiture of Pompey as a member of the hated 'triumvirate'. Even on Cicero's own showing, he had had warning enough. In 59 first Cicero's colleague M. Antonius, then the ex-governor of Asia, L. Valerius Flaccus, who as praetor in 63 had been of use to Cicero, were prosecuted. Antonius was condemned – a tribute to Catiline from his unregenerate supporters, claims Cicero: they raised an altar in his honour and held a feast. Flaccus was luckier – acquitted by the senators and *equites* who had backed Cicero in 63. Cicero (prophetically) told the court that he too was under a threat and would meet it even in a popular assembly.

Clodius in 58, having shed his patrician rank and become tribune of the plebs, was vindicating the rights and liberties of the Roman People, not only against the optimates but in open rivalry with the 'triumvirs', who were in his view fake *populares*. Clodius was ingenious. He brought in a bill that ordered any person who had been responsible for the death of Roman citizens without trial should suffer the penalty of exile, in the form of deprivation of the right to water and fire: anyone under that interdict could be killed on sight. The cleverness of this measure was that it obviated the need for any form of trial, at which Cicero's oratorical skill, so effective in begging off his clients, would be deployed to the full on his own behalf. Cicero had to leave Italy and his house on the Palatine Hill was razed. None of the 'triumvirs' would help him; the consuls A. Gabinius and L. Piso boasted of their connexions with Catiline and Cethegus, and the optimates professed themselves unable to act against Clodius. Cicero rightly regarded himself as betrayed. Yet given the bargain he had once struck, and men with whom he struck it, he could hardly have expected anything else. It was not until the following year, when Clodius had gone out of office, that the consul of 57, P. Cornelius Lentulus Spinther, was able to get the Senate to vote for the recall of Rome's civilian saviour. Meanwhile someone was decorating Catiline's grave with flowers.

7

Historiography and Villainy

Cicero's speeches, letters, and memoirs

First call for enquirers into the Catilinarian conspiracy must be the purposefully mendacious and self-serving speeches of Cicero himself (who in his dialogue *Brutus* makes Atticus say that orators were allowed to lie if it helped their case). A. W. Lintott distinguishes two types of misrepresentation: the brief and unadorned lie introduced into the mass of the text, whatever the status of that text, using the 'fibs' that Cicero's treatise *On the Orator* claimed should season a speech, and 'falsehood by implication through tendentious description'. There is more though, as Lintott insists, than questions of the veracity of the speeches and of the texts as we have them and their relation to what was actually uttered: there is controversy about the extent to which such texts represent anything that could have been delivered in a Roman court.

In 60 Cicero published a collection of speeches he had delivered during his consulship. The publication of speeches was nothing to mock. Great orators did it, and went on doing it, even into the Principate. Speeches delivered in a losing cause were specially worth giving a second hearing. Cicero's collection arguably, but not indisputably, comprised those he delivered in the Senate on 1 January and to the People on the Rullan Bill, one in defence of the tribune Otho and his regulation of theatre seating, one for Rabirius, one against

110 Catiline

the restoration of privileges to sons of men proscribed by Sulla, one in which Cicero explained to the People his refusal of a province, the four orations against Catiline, and two (brief) on the agrarian bill. Eight survive in whole or part. The original orations were delivered from notes, or even in part *ex tempore,* and Cicero naturally edited them to improve the arguments and fit the context more suitably. At the extreme, A. W. Lintott describes the fourth Catilinarian as 'a cento', perhaps 'largely a fiction', whose themes fit the period after the consulship when Cicero's stand needed defence. The classics we have are not verbatim accounts of what he said, and in any case would already need the sharp scrutiny that they have been undergoing for more than a century, not only for what they include but for what they leave out. Even later, writing in 56 to the historian L. Lucceius about a proposed monograph on his consulship, he urged that it was not necessary to keep to the strict truth.

It might well be said that Catiline owed his lasting fame to Cicero's efforts to spread his own. More than that, he perpetuated two images of Catiline. The man whose criminal career began in his adolescence served to carry the crimes of others, if Cicero needed to unload them. But Cicero also depicted the villain with superficially redeeming features whose protégé M. Caelius Rufus, Cicero's client in 56, had once been. This is the man who takes over at the end of Sallust's monograph, dying like a soldier.

Of the ancient commentaries on the speeches, the prime is that of Q. Asconius Pedianus, a knowledgeable and inquiring writer (d. AD 76) who worked on forensic speeches and the electoral address of 64. Of the third- and fourth-century commentators the best known is the 'Bobbio Scholiast' after the monastery in Piacenza in which the manuscript of his work was found; it is useful for his commentary on Cicero's speech in defence of Sulla.

Then comes the correspondence. Cicero's letters to his friend Atticus start in 68 and go on until November 44. They are

Historiography and Villainy

comparatively candid, but allusive and intermittent. There is a small batch to his brother (*Ad Q. Fratrem*), overwhelmed in bulk by guarded, sometimes deceitful letters to friends (*Ad familiares, Ad M. Brutum*), which take us from 62 to 43.

Cicero also commemorated his own achievements. By March of 60 he had written a sketch (*Commentary*) in Greek and was thinking of one in Latin, as well as a poem 'On my consulship'. Another poem, on his exile, pro-Ciceronian, was completed in three books in 54 and called 'On my own Times'; Caesar did not care for its first book. The memoir helps to account for the pro-Ciceronian tendencies of later Greek writers such as Plutarch and Cassius Dio. Nothing came of Lucceius' pro-Ciceronian monograph, and the memoir on his political strategy that Cicero wrote after the deaths of Crassus, Pompey and Caesar is known only from references to it in later writers. The pamphlet called *Advice on Electioneering* purports to be written by Cicero's brother Quintus for the campaign of 64. It is more likely a rhetorical study from a later time, but A. W. Lintott, like others, is willing to accept it as a work written to create or confirm support for the ostensible recipient.

Sallust's monograph

C. Sallustius Crispus is one of the two eminent Roman historians to be known in English-speaking countries by an anglicized version of his name, the other being the great Livy. The *War Against Catiline* was his first work and seems to have been written as the Second Triumvirate was formed and carried out its murders and confiscations: 42–41. The author was born in at Sabine Amiternum (San Vittorino) in about 86 BC, into a well-off family. He was a product of the enfranchisement of Italy and suffered from that origin, as did his contemporaries who embarked on a political career in the savage competitiveness of the period. Such men had a choice, one that Cicero made as he reached the natural ceiling of a new man's career. He must either espouse the *status quo* as the morally irreproachable Cato the Censor had done in the first half of the second century BC and, with ability and luck, become a pillar of the establishment, or press for greater openness and for reforms, taking up the popular cause whenever it emerged. Sallust took the second line and attached himself to Julius Caesar. In 52 he was tribune of the plebs and a member of the board that enacted the bill that gave Caesar, away in Gaul, the controversial right to stand for the consulship in absence. Two years later he was expelled from the senate by optimate censors, on the standard charge of immorality. When civil war broke out a few months later he fought on Caesar's side as commander of a legion and was rewarded with a praetorship in 46, followed up with a proconsulship in Africa, where he had fought. It was a significant posting: Africa was productive and tempting; besides, Caesar's opponents had put up a strong resistance to him there, and the younger Cato's suicide at Utica left a deep impression that was to last for generations. Sallust's governorship was not a success; he was accused of extortion, whether justly or perhaps for political or personal reasons. Either way, Caesar is said to have saved him from conviction. It is to be hoped that that charge was baseless, given the diatribe against the prime offence of greed that he delivered in his account of moral decline at the beginning of the *War Against Catiline.*

Sallust retired into private life and devoted himself, as he tells us, rather defensively, to the study of history. (Former) politicians were thought to be particularly well qualified to expound it, and Thucydides, Sallust and Tacitus still command veneration. Ronald Syme famously used the phrase 'the consular historian' to stress the authority of Tacitus. Sallust never reached the consulship, even in the troubled years of the 'Second' Triumvirate. He was a man of the past and died in about 35, leaving his *Histories* of the post-Sullan period

Historiography and Villainy 113

unfinished. Before going on to his major work, Sallust completed another monograph, the *War Against Jugurtha*, which also dealt with politics, this time in the troubled post-Gracchan age towards the end of the second century; it showed up popular politicians as venal as their opponents.

It was once held that Sallust wrote his monograph as an answer to Cicero's posthumous, and lost memoir on his political strategy. What is known about this work is that Cicero, after the deaths of both Crassus and Caesar, accused them of involvement in the Catilinarian conspiracy. It would be good to know how far Cicero went with these charges, from a simple claim that Catiline's campaigns for the consulship were encouraged or funded by them, to outright approval and support for the rising. This theory of Sallust's aims has been abandoned. They were not so narrow, and his villain Catiline is his own man. Sallust does implicitly exonerate Caesar, but he does justice to Cicero too, and there is no trace of irony in his calling Cicero, conventionally enough, 'the excellent consul'.

Sallust's strong moral stance, and his conception of decline from an ideal past, which was shared by many ancient historians and thinkers, notably by Livy, made him essentially a social conservative. His career made it natural for him to blame the ruling class, especially the aristocratic cliques that expected honours as a right and used office to manipulate the political system and their inferiors, increasing their own wealth and power still further. This phenomenon went well back beyond the Sullan period to the time of Jugurtha (118–104) who bribed alike the generals sent against him and the tribunals set up at Rome by popular politicians to judge his case. The *Catiline* showed corruption at work in later generations. Sallust was personally involved and knew the men he brought on: Pompey, Cicero, Cato and Caesar, perhaps Catiline himself. Personal impressions counted, and oral testimony, and in his presentation of the debate on the conspirators Cicero is given an honourable but not a brilliant place: that is assigned to the speeches of Caesar and Cato. Sallust contrasts their characters, explicitly and in their speeches, doing both full justice. Sallust has no doubt at all of the guilt of all the conspirators, Catiline, Lentulus Sura, and the manifestly guilty Manlius. They were intent on overthrowing the power of the men who were living off the Sullan constitution as it was embodied in the ruling oligarchy and on achieving their own supremacy. Sallust does not elaborate on their long-term aims, not surprisingly, as they will have been various and probably ill-formed. Social reform was included, though only in the limited form of the abolition of debt.

Catiline was no idealist, seeking reform for its own sake, but only another L. Apuleius Saturninus, or (as Sallust might later have reflected) another Clodius, seeking to remedy a setback in his career. That made Sallust receptive to the arguments of Cicero and to the drastic measures that Cicero took against the conspirators. His work reflects the Ciceronian point of view and indeed describes the 'first Catilinarian' speech, which scholars have found so unsatisfactory, as 'brilliant and valuable'. Nonetheless he admits that some items he records (notably the scandals about Catiline's early life) may have been malicious fictions.

This had serious consequences. Sallust has no notion of Catiline as a man undecided about his actions until the last minute. Even worse, he is shown – as Caesar too has been shown – aiming at supremacy right from the end of Sulla's dictatorship and caring nothing for the way he attained it, provided he secured a tyranny for himself. Sallust uses the word *regnum*, kingship, a word reserved in Latin for the goal of men who aimed at seizing for themselves the one-man government of the early monarchy at Rome, especially that of the Tarquins. Right from his adolescence Catiline hankered after civil war, slaughter, looting and civil discord, and it was on this that he spent his youth. His natural aggression was simply driven, as time went on, by a desperate shortage of funds and, as Sallust adds, the burden of guilt. All this took place against the general background of declining morality, of the luxury and greed that Sallust excoriates. His picture presents without hesitation a man who planned revolution for 17 years before attempting it. That is unacceptable, and even the inclusion of Catiline in the 'conspiracy' of 66–65 was a fiction.

Sallust was not a 'consular historian' but he was greatly admired by the supreme Cornelius Tacitus. In the *Annals* Tacitus describes him as 'a' (or 'the') most distinguished writer on Roman History. Tacitus, like Sallust, was as concerned with style as he was with content, and this remark may be intended as praise of the author's elegance and effectiveness. Sallust in turn was an admirer of Thucydides' austere, elliptical, sometimes obscure manner, and, among Latin writers, of the archaism of Cato the Censor. Sallust's own style had other admirers than Tacitus. The historian L. Arruntius, writing under Augustus, slavishly followed mannerisms that made him a laughing stock to the Younger Seneca, who treated him in a *Letter* of the early 60s AD as representative of an entire school, for 'truncated epigrams, words that take the reader unawares, baffling brevity'.

Roman historians of the Principate

Sallust's fame and authority made his account of the conspiracy the received one, not to be challenged until the nineteenth century. Of Livy – whose history, written in the principate of Augustus, would have been informative, if not penetrating – we have only abbreviated versions, *Periochae*, which have brought his account into modern times. Book 102 summarizes the Catilinarian conspiracy in three sentences that express the received view:

> Having suffered two defeats in his candidature for the consulship he conspired with the praetor Lentulus and Cethegus and a large

116   *Catiline*

number of others to slaughter consuls and Senate, fire the City, and bring the Republic to an end, an army also having been prepared in Etruria. That conspiracy was eradicated by the conscientious efforts of Cicero. After Catiline had been driven from the City the remaining conspirators paid the penalty.

Whether Livy's original binds Catiline and the other conspirators to Manlius' rising, as the *Periocha* suggests, is unclear. Another work derived from Livy, Julius Obsequens' fourth-century *Book of Prodigies*, provides examples of the portents that led to 'the abominable conspiracy of Catiline'. How Catiline haunted Roman historians is clear from evident references to him in the early part of Livy's *History*, not merely in a verbal catch used by Cicero to open his first speech against Catiline and by later writers: 'How long are you going to look at me so expectantly?' Livy puts this into the mouth of a doomed champion of the plebs, M. Manlius Capitolinus, in 384 BC. In Livy's treatment it is part of Capitolinus' whole Catiline-inspired conspiracy.

Velleius Paterculus, loyal Italian officer of the conservative Emperor Tiberius and praetor of AD 15, who produced his brief history in AD 30, was not the man to offer novel interpretations of the Catilinarian conspiracy. Rather, he devotes several lines to praise of Cicero, an intellectual genius who like himself was a 'new man', owed all his success to himself and displayed extraordinary courage, steadiness, vigilance and attention. Nonetheless, scholars have not failed to notice the closeness of features of Sallust's portrait to Tacitus' of the Emperor Tiberius' sinister minister L. Aelius Sejanus (c. 20 BC–AD 31), who wormed his way into the Emperor's confidence and was finally struck down for his attacks on members of the imperial family, which were taken to imply conspiring against the Emperor himself. Certainly Tiberius feared him at the end. So even the laudatory portrait painted by Velleius, which was published at the height of Sejanus' power, just before he fell, shares some of Catiline's preternatural, almost demonic

Historiography and Villainy

traits. For Sallust finishes off his portrait by presenting Catiline as a near-madman, specifically after the murder of his son. Guilt gave him no rest sleeping or waking and brought on his crime. The diagnosis exempts the historian from rational analysis.

The stereotype continued in Latin historical writing into the early second century, when L. Annaeus Florus produced his *Epitome of Roman History*, based on Livy. He included a chapter on the conspiracy, full of indignant rhetorical flights. He cannot resist, though, the final flourish on the courage of the rebels, who died to a man in the places assigned to them – except that Catiline was out in front surrounded by the bodies of his enemies: a glorious death, if he had met it on behalf of his country. By the time we reach Eutropius, an imperial official active in the second half of the fourth century who wrote a ten-book compendium of Roman history dependent on an *Epitome* of Livy, the material has become very exiguous: only the essential high birth of the desperadoes, their death by strangulation, Catiline's on the battlefield, remain.

Greek writers

A few scraps had already been contributed by Diodorus of Sicily in his universal *Library of History*, written at the end of the Republic. Most interesting is the biographer and philosopher Plutarch (L. Mestrius Plutarchus, c. 46–120), another writer domesticated by English readers. He was a native of Chaeronea in Boeotia, but a Roman citizen and learned in Roman lore and history. The main material comes from his biography of Cicero and from his later lives of Caesar, Cato the Younger and Crassus. Plutarch aptly balanced his *Cicero* with his life of Demosthenes, who in the fourth century BC spoke up for the freedom of Athens against the encroachment of Philip of Macedon, and, like Cicero in his struggle against the Triumvir

Antony, ultimately died for his beliefs. Plutarch is sympathetic to Cicero, and made use of his Greek commentary on his consulship, which he knew first-hand, even for his account of the crimes of Catiline's youth. He antedates the conspiracy to 64, like Sallust, so explaining aristocratic support for Cicero. But there were other sources, perhaps Livy. It is a persuasive hypothesis of C. R. B. Pelling that the draft on which Plutarch based his *Cicero* was also used for his later biographies, but with varied deployment of the material. Favourable as he is to his heroes, Plutarch does not ignore their weaknesses. Catiline by contrast is a ready-made out-and-out villain.

Next comes the mid-second-century historian Appian, from Asia Minor or Alexandria (c. 95–165), who wrote a history of Rome and her wars, notably the Civil Wars, down to 35 BC. Here again there is little deviation from the stereotype and its lurid details, apart from putting the proposal of Ti. Nero before that of Caesar, and making the latter suggest imprisonment only until the defeat of Catiline, to be followed by a regular trial. Appian's desperate Catiline, the killer of his own son, was aiming at the consulship only as a step towards tyranny; and he has women who wanted to be rid of their husbands subscribing funds to the rising. Appian notes the distinctions conferred on Cicero, who was now taken for a man of action, specially the title 'Father of his Country' used by Cato, which Appian connects with the designation of emperors, conferred as a matter of course as soon as they could be made out to have earned it.

A full account of the conspiracy in Greek is that of Cassius Dio (c. 155–235), a senator of Bithynian origin, who wrote under the Severan dynasty in the earlier years of the third century. Unfortunately Dio is only as good as his sources; he too for this period goes back to Livy.

Historiography and Villainy   119

Literary descendants of Catiline

Sallust's portrait of Catiline rapidly became influential as a literary paradigm of villainy, passing into poetry from historical writing with all the literary freedom that a double removal from reality allows. For in the *Aeneid* Virgil (70–19) has him depicted on Aeneas' shield, 'hanging in Tartarus from a threatening rock and trembling at the faces of the Furies'.

With Catiline established as a paradigm of villainy it is no surprise to find him mentioned as one of the specimens of remarkable behaviour brought out by the moralizing writer Valerius Maximus, a near contemporary of Velleius, who brings in evidence the poisoning of Catiline's only grown son to forward his own marriage. For the same paradigmatic reason he figures in world history as it was recounted in the handy volumes of late antiquity, such as the *Seven Books of History against the Pagans* by the Spanish priest Orosius (early fifth century). So the story of Catiline was passed on to the Renaissance.

Catiline on the stage

In England the standard version was propagated for a wider audience on the stage in 1611 when Ben Jonson, following at a distance of least 14 years in the footsteps of the Elizabethan puritan Stephen Gosson (1574–1624), one of whose lost plays was *Catilins Conspiracies,* put on *Catiline His Conspiracy.* This was the second of two pieces with which Jonson intended to make his name; curiously enough, the first was *Seianus His Fall,* of 1603. *Catiline* was booed off, but gained in popularity later and lasted on the stage for a century or so. Since then it has had countless readers. The political subject engendered many other stage works, including some by celebrated European writers: Voltaire (1754), who makes Cicero claim that if he had been in charge of Catiline he would have turned out like Scipio; Grillparzer (1822); Dumas (1848), who opens with young Catiline having a son by a Vestal; Ibsen (1857), who is concerned with the relationship of the individual to society and the need for purity in reformers. By the end of the nineteenth century there were nearly 40 items. To crown it all, there are operas: one by Salieri (1792) to a 'dramma tragicomico' by Giambattista Casti; another by the Scottish composer Iain Hamilton, *The Catiline Conspiracy* of 1973. No librettist is named; the composer seems to have used the traditional material, giving Fulvia and Sempronia enhanced roles. In the manner of Shakespeare (and with historical insight) Hamilton brings on the ghost of Sulla, as Ben Jonson had done, and a spectre of Caesar at Pistoria. More recently still, Catiline has emerged in a favourite modern genre: Steven Saylor's *Catilina's Riddle* is *A Mystery of Ancient Rome* (London, 1992) – one of his 'Roma sub Rosa' series, and a product of research as well as of imagination.

Rehabilitation

Sallust had cut Catiline's portrait in durable stone. It was only long after the Renaissance and Enlightenment, after the French Revolution and the spread of radical politics throughout Europe that rival interpretations were offered. Napoleon I and III both favoured Catiline, not surprisingly, considering the 'Caesarism' of both emperors. Of course it had always been possible to have things both ways, to hold a conventional view of Catiline and still to execrate Cicero: this had been the purpose of the unknown author of the pseudo-Sallustian *Invective against Cicero*, a work that may belong to the Augustan age but is written as if from a perspective of ten years after the conspiracy; the stance is taken up in the *History* of Cassius Dio.

Most notable in modern times is E. S. Beesly's *Catiline, Clodius, and Tiberius,* published in London in 1878. Beesly was Professor of History at University College in the University of London and a friend of Karl Marx. He fought for an independent working-class trade-union movement, supporting the Amalgamated Society of Carpenters and Joiners, and was prominent in the anti-slavery movement. His efforts were met by attempts to unseat 'Professor Beestly'. Beesly's study of Catiline, which followed some favourable judgements made 12 years earlier by Napoleon III in his *Histoire de Jules César,* liberated enquiry and polarized scholarship: was Catiline the villain, or rather Cicero, who framed him for his own purposes? Such discussions, already refined by the analysis of Zvi Yavetz, who found four presentations – the villain, the social reformer, the victim of factional struggles, and the backer of indebted Italian aristocrats – have not been laid to rest by the work of Waters and Phillips. The compulsion to vindicate a villain has led to an implausible theory that Sallust's account of Catiline's courageous end was used by the first-century AD Greek writer on generalship, Onasander, for a eulogy of Catiline as a model general.

The thesis of this book is that we have a set of politicians who were victims of the conventions of their city and forced to play a political game that was governed by long-standing rules. Those rules favoured birth and wealth, and a man who was disadvantaged had to manipulate, or sometimes break, the rules to make his way. Cicero, to win his longed-for consulship, had to make a pact which meant bringing on and exposing whatever discontent he could find. He broke the law but stayed faithful to his undertaking. The irony was that his action led only to more dissent and disruption. Pompey in his political eclipse of 61–60 used an alliance with a dynamic and unscrupulous incoming consul to get his own way, as he had previously used tribunes.

When a direct conflict arose between conformity and ambition and a choice to be made, both Catiline and Caesar chose to end the game altogether and, if necessary, destroy the existing constitution rather than give up their own cause. That was not their intention, despite what Plutarch and others say about Catiline's plan to destroy the whole government and cause complete chaos; rather they meant to vindicate their own position in regular government. Catiline was like Pompey and even more like Caesar. Defeated by the optimates in the game of politics, they did not accept their defeat but used whatever other weapons they had at their disposal to reverse it. Catiline, instead of going tamely into exile when his career was at an end, turned to Manlius in Etruria and backed his rebellion, hoping that he might turn success in Italy into an alliance with Pompey. Caesar, more intelligent and more resourceful, was outmanoeuvred in 50 and had no further legal defence for his retention of his full army while he stood for another consulship. He took to outright civil war; but he had ten legions in top form to follow him.

How serious was Catiline's plan of reform? The man himself claimed to have taken up the cause of the destitute, and that that was his practice. If we do not hear of concrete proposals, that may be because we are not allowed to hear of them. All we hear of is vague accusations of revolution, in particular the abolition of debt. When Caesar came to power as Dictator in 48, two measures he put in place were the relief (not the abolition) of debt and the long-delayed restoration of political rights to the sons of men proscribed by Sulla. Nothing of that is known to have figured in Catiline's programme, but on his own showing it should have. The 'programme' was exiguous and subordinated to Catiline's plans for himself, his senatorial allies, and his junior henchmen.

How far back did 'conspiracy' stretch? According to Cicero, speaking in 63, it began in 64; when he spoke in 62 it went back three years, or two, depending on his purpose. He did not scruple to adjust the timing and he misled historians. Leaving aside Cicero's purposes, and mere talk among leaderless groups in the lower strata of society, we must adjust this: only the consular elections of 63 and the defeat

Historiography and Villainy

of Catiline marked the beginning of a distinctively Catilinarian revolution.

The basis of this work is that Catiline and the other two protagonists, Cicero and Pompey, were all victims of a militaristic slave state which saw its subjects too as slaves. To ensure dominance, well-defined and strictly enforced rules were imposed for status and advancement. Politicians were playing a game according to those rules, keeping their inordinate rivalry in check (so it was hoped).

If politics was a game, where was the morality in it? It rested in practising the 'virtues' that benefited the Res Publica: courage in the field (*virtus*, manliness, itself) and self-control and abstinence. Greed and extravagance in the public and private sphere undermined stability by giving one individual undue advantages. We may, if we like, buy into this scheme, accepting conventional views of right and wrong at Rome, or we may persist in seeing it in a less rosy light as the creation of that militaristic state. Fears began near the beginning of the second century with the successes of Roman generals in the east and the influx of wealth from their conquests. For moderns this centring on the Respublica is inadequate. It leaves aside the attitude of the Respublica itself towards the rights of its neighbours and subjects. (We began at the siege of Rome's 'ally' Asculum.) More relevantly, it leaves aside the lives of the underprivileged (to say nothing of the slave population). Stability meant restricting their demands for more land, grain, water, and protection against fire and flood. The remedies for these ills were clear, but only inadequately addressed, and hardly ever without controversy and violence. This was where weakness was embedded in the Roman system: unwillingness to allow any individual to win special credit by bringing in measures in their favour. Commissions of enquiry followed by united action would have been the solution, not individual and corporate self-seeking. These problems were only, and then partially, solved when control finally passed into the hands of one man, Augustus. The young men at the siege of Asculum were subscribers to the system, defective though it was. They all damaged it. Cicero was defending it, but his execution of the Catilinarians raised serious issues, as A. Drummond succinctly put it, of the interaction between law and politics and the protection of individual liberties. Catiline, Pompey and Caesar were all blatantly guilty, Pompey more subtly than Caesar, as Tacitus remarked when he compared the last two: Pompey was more covert, not less culpable. Catiline, with his '*vastus animus*', exposes the type most clearly, through lacking their talents. The word *vastus* does not mean merely large: it has connotations of greed, insatiability and desolation. It was fitting for him to be portrayed by Virgil tormented by the Furies and by Lucan attempting to seize the Elysian Fields.

Further Reading

For the parallel of Guy Fawkes, see A. Fraser, *The Gunpowder Plot: Terror and Faith in 1605* (London, 1997). False dichotomies: D. Hackett-Fischer, *Historians' Fallacies: Towards a Logic of Historical Thought* (New York, 1970). E. G. Hardy, *The Catilinarian Conspiracy in its Context: A Re-study of the Evidence* (Oxford, 1924) made a thorough study.

Literature on the economic, social and political development of Italy in the second and first centuries BC is vast and controversial. A view based on Appian and Plutarch, of the increasing dominance of vast estates run by rich landowners with slave labour, entailing depopulation and a shortage of respectable manpower for the legions, was represented by P. A. Brunt, *Italian Manpower 225 BC–AD 14* (Oxford, 1971, 2nd edn, 1987) and K. Hopkins, *Death and Renewal* (Cambridge, 1983). A different interpretation of the evidence came with the pioneering article of J. W. Rich, 'The supposed Roman manpower shortage of the later second century BC', *Historia* 32 (1983): 287–331, and more recently in his paper 'Tiberius Gracchus, Land, and Manpower' in *Crises and the Roman Empire: Proceedings of the Seventh Workshop of the International Network Impact of Empire*, O. Hekster, G. de Kleijn and D. Slootjes (eds) (Leiden, 2007). A recent work argues convincingly for a moderate view: S. Hin, *The Population of Roman Italy: Population Dynamics in an Ancient Conquest Society 201 BCE–14 CE* (New York, 2013). For Roman democracy, see F. G. B. Millar, *The Crowd in Rome in the Late Republic* (Ann Arbor, 1998). Polybius' view is set out in his *Histories*, Book 6; the debate continues.

Pompey and Catiline at Asculum are attested in H. Dessau, *Inscriptiones Latinae Selectae* (Berlin, 1916), 8888, with L. R. Taylor,

126   *Further Reading*

The Voting Districts of the Roman Republic (Rome, 1960), 177. On their careers, see for Pompey R. Seager, *Pompey the Great* (Oxford, 2002); for Cicero there are two volumes by T. N. Mitchell, *The Ascending Years* and *The Senior Statesman* (New Haven and London, 1979 and 1991); D. L. Stockton's *Political Biography* (Oxford, 1971), and E. D. Rawson's *Portrait* (Harmondsworth, 1975; repr. Bristol, 1983); the latter has a sharper focus on Cicero's intellectual interests. M. Licinius Crassus lurks in the background of Catiline's story; he is given body by A. M. Ward in his *Marcus Crassus and the Late Roman Republic* (Columbia and London, c. 1977). For minor players see E. Badian, 'The early career of A. Gabinius', *Philologus* 103 (1959): 87–99, and J. Linderski, 'Cicero and Sallust on Vargunteius', *Historia* 12 (1963): 511f. The *Oxford Classical Dictionary*, 4th edn, S. Hornblower, A. Spawforth and S. Eidinow (2012) remains as helpful as ever.

Political integration and problems of land tenure for Italians in different regions are cogently discussed by R. Stewart, 'Catiline and the crisis of 63–60: the Italian Perspective', *Latomus* 54 (1995): 62–8. For currency shortage and credit crisis in provincial context, see M. H. Crawford, *Coinage and Money under the Roman Republic* (Cambridge, 1985), 192f., 240f.; continuing crises are discussed by M. W. Frederiksen in 'Caesar, Cicero, and the problem of debt', *Journal of Roman Studies* 56 (1966): 128–41. E. S. Gruen, in his magisterial survey of the leading conspirators in *The Last Generation of the Roman Republic* (Berkeley, Los Angeles and London, 1975) 120–132, is inclined to play it down as a stimulus for discontented aristocrats, as compared with loss of face. As to disaffected youth, E. Isayeva, 'Unruly youth? The myth of generation conflict in the late Roman Republic', *Historia* 56 (2007): 1–13 attempts to bring down its significance.

For the proscriptions and Catiline's role, see B. Marshall, 'Catilina and the execution of M. Marius Gratidianus', *Classical Quarterly*

35 (1985): 124–33. He underwent other trials, notably for violating a Vestal: T. J. Cadoux, 'Catiline and the Vestal Virgins', *Historia* 54 (2005): 162–79.

When it comes to the so-called 'first Catilinarian conspiracy', R. Seager elucidates its build-up most convincingly, in the paper he names after it in *Historia* 13 (1964): 338–47. E. S. Gruen, 'Notes on the "first Catilinarian conspiracy"', *Classical Philology* 64 (1969): 20–4, detaches Catiline and Cn. Piso from the electoral struggles: Manilius was the issue. For the sequence of events, see E. J. Phillips, 'Cicero and the prosecution of C. Manilius', *Latomus* 29 (1970): 595–607; J. T. Ramsey, 'The Prosecution of C. Manilius in 66 BC and Cicero's *Pro Manilio*', *Phoenix* 34 (1980): 323–36. Like some other scholars, C. E. Stevens in 'The "Plotting" of BC 66/65', *Latomus* 22 (1963): 397–435, argued that the conspiracy was part of an ongoing scheme devised by Pompey's enemies to neutralize him when he returned victorious from the east.

As to the year of revolution, 63, T. P. Wiseman in the *Cambridge Ancient History* 9 (2nd edn, 1995), 346–67, has a vivid account in context. For religious aspects he discusses 'Lucretius, Catiline, and the survival of prophecy', in his *Historiography and Imagination: Eight Essays on Roman Culture* (Exeter, 1994), 49–67. The trial of Rabirius is well discussed by Lintott 2008, 120–2.

Sceptical analysis of a 'Catilinarian' conspiracy began in English with E. S. Beesly, *Catiline, Clodius, and Tiberius* (London, 1878), 1–37. It was vigorously taken up by K. Waters, 'Cicero, Sallust, and Catiline', *Historia* 19 (1970): 195–215; by R. Seager, 'Iusta Catilinae', *Historia* 22 (1973): 240–8; and by T. Loposzko, 'The Malversations of the Consul Cicero', *Mélanges T. Kotula Antiquitas* 18 (Wroclaw, 1993). In defence of Cicero and against any 'left wing' interpretation there appeared E. J. Phillips, 'Catiline's conspiracy', *Historia* 25 (1976): 441–8. Phillips' claim that Cicero can be faulted only for his exploitation of the 'first Catilinarian conspiracy', for making Lentulus the ringleader at Laeca's house, and for implicating Crassus after his death misses the main point: the executions.

Why the conspiracy failed: a classic paper is Z. Yavetz's, 'The failure of Catiline's conspiracy', *Historia* 12 (1963): 485–99. Reasons for Cicero's choice of conspirators to bring before the Senate: D. A. March, 'Cicero and the "Gang of Five"', *Classical World* 82.4 (1989): 225–34. On the legality of the proceedings, A. Drummond, *Law, Politics, and Power: Sallust and the Execution of the Catilinarian Conspirators*, Hist. Einzelschr. 93 (Stuttgart, 1995) was thorough and convincing.

The decisive role of the Senate in dealing with the Italian uprising is insisted on by Stewart (1995), cited above. For the chronology of the campaign of Pistoria, see G. V. Sumner, 'The last journey of L. Sergius Catilina', *Classical Philology* 58 (1963): 215–19, and for the speed of news on the road: N. J. E. Austin and B. Rankov, *Exploration: Military and Political Intelligence in the Roman World from the Second Punic War until the Battle of Adrianople* (London, 1995), 124f.

For Clodius as Catiline's natural successor: see A. W. Lintott, 'P. Clodius Pulcher – *Felix Catilina?*', *Greece and Rome* NS 14 (1967): 157–69. The 'Bona Dea affair', the subject of a host of articles, is perhaps best approached in the sober pages of T. P. Wiseman, *Cambridge Ancient History* 9 (2nd edn, 1995), or in the *Oxford Classical Dictionary* (above).

Most of the ancient works, sources for Catiline and the first century BC, can be read in English in Loeb or Penguin translations. A collection of all the literary evidence, but with translations into German, was made by H. Drexler (Darmstadt, 1976). The quotes used in this book have been adapted from the Loeb translations.

Cicero's *Catilinarians* have been edited with useful introductions and notes by A. R. Dyck (Cambridge, 2008), with J. J. Price offering stringent comments on 'The failure of Cicero's "first Catilinarian"' in *Studies in Latin Literature and Roman History* 9 (1998): 106–28.

Further Reading   129

D. H. Berry's edition of Cicero's *Pro P. Sulla Oratio*, Cambridge Classical Texts and Commentaries 30 (Cambridge, 1996) has commentary and introduction and valuable remarks on the 'first conspiracy'. Cicero's *Letters* (*To Atticus* and *To his Friends*) have been edited and the former translated by D. R. Shackleton-Bailey (10 vols, Cambridge, 1965–80). For Cicero as a guide to historians, A. W. Lintott, *Cicero as Evidence: A Historian's Companion* (Oxford, 2008) is illuminating and indispensable, especially 16–32 on the texts of the speeches and 33–42 on veracity; 13–35 Cicero's speech as a candidate and the pamphlet *On Electioneering*; 136 on the 'consular' speeches; 142–81 speeches against Catiline. As to his attack on Crassus, E. D. Rawson assessed that in *Liverpool Classical Monthly* 7/8 (82): 121–4, and her 'History, Historiography, and Cicero's *Expositio Consiliorum suorum*' reappeared in her *Collected Papers* (Oxford, 1991), 408–15.

Asconius is the most important ancient commentator on Cicero: for his contribution see B. A. Marshall, *A Historical Commentary on Asconius* (Columbia, Missouri, 1985) and R. G. Lewis, revised by J. Harries, *Asconius: Commentaries on Speeches by Cicero*, translated by R. G. Lewis, revised by J. Harries et al. (Oxford, 2006).

For Sallust's *Catiline* the edition with commentary by P. McGushin (Bristol, 1980) is helpful; he had already published a separate commentary (Leiden, 1977), while T. J. Ramsey's *Sallust's Bellum Catilinae* (New York, 1984) has now come out in a second edition (2007). R. Syme's study of the historian's career and work (Oxford, 1964) remains a classic. For Sallust's view on the destruction of conspiracies, see D. Shewen, 'Sallust and Cato the Censor', *Classical Quarterly* 50 (2000): 70–91.

Plutarch the literary scholar is shown at work by C. B. R. Pelling, 'Plutarch and Catiline', a paper from *Hermes* 113 (1985): 311–29 and republished in *Plutarch and History, Eighteen Studies* (Swansea, 2002), 45–64.

For the many dramas on the subject of Catiline, see H. B. G. Speck, *Katilina im Drama der Weltliteratur: Ein Beitrag zur vergleichenden Stoffgeschichte des Römerdramas 1597–1905* (Leipzig, 1906). Most of them take us back to 'Catiline's "ravaged mind": Vastus animus (Sall. *Cat.* 5. 5)', see C. B. Krebs, *Class. Quarterly* 58 (2008): 682–6.

Index

Advice on Electioneering (Cicero, Quintus) 111
Aeneid (Virgil) 4, 119
Allobroges, the 73–8
Annius Chilo, Q. 56
Antonius, M. 31, 40, 41, 82, 84, 106
Antony, Mark 105
Apennines, the 48
Appian 118
Apulia (Puglie) 48
Arruntius, L. 115
Asconius Pedianus, Q. 110
Asculum (Ascoli Piceno) 1
assassination 64–5
Augustus, Emperor 95, 105
Aurelia 101, 102

Beesly, E. S. 121
    Catiline, Clodius, and Tiberius 121
Book of Prodigies (Obsequens, Julius) 116
Bruttium (Calabria) 48

Caecilius, Q. 24–5
Caecilius Metellus, Q. 82
Caeparius, M. of Tarracina (Terracina) 48
Caesar, Gaius Julius 32–4, 89, 102, 122
    Catilinarian Conspiracy of 63 and 44, 65, 78, 80–1
    Crassus, M. Licinius and 104–5
    Pompeius, Gnaeus 'Pompey' ('the Great') and 91, 104–5
Calenus, C. Fufius 103
Calpurnius Bestia, L. 56, 72–3
Campania 47–8
Capito, Publius Gabinius 4, 56
Capua 61

Cassius Dio 118, 120
Cassius Longinus, L. 55
Catilinarian Conspiracy of 63 44–6
    Allobroges, and the 73–8
    areas affected 46–9
    Catiline (Lucius Sergius) and 54, 63–9, 70, 72, 82–5
    Cicero, Marcus Tullius and 45–6, 63–7, 69–70, 73, 81–3
    conspirators and 54–8, 70–7, 80–2
    Crassus letters and 63–5
    debt and 58–9
    Etruria and 59–61
    executions and 80–2
    military resources and 49–50, 51
    Pistoria, Battle of 83–5
    Senate, and the 61–2
Catilina's Riddle (Saylor, Steven) 120
Catiline (Lucius Sergius) 121–2, 124
    Catilinarian Conspiracy of 63 54, 63–9, 70, 72, 82–5 *see also* Catilinarian Conspiracy of 63
    death of 83–5
    departure from Rome 65–9, 70
    'first Catilinarian conspiracy' 35–40
    Gratidianus, M. Marius and 24, 27
    heritage of 4–5
    marriages of 27–8
    money and 28–9
    murders and 23–5, 27, 31
    personality 5–7
    politics and 2, 13, 27, 28–31, 50–4
    Pompeius, Gnaeus 'Pompey' ('the Great') and 91–4
    Sallust and 114–15
    sexual offences and 26–7
    trial for extortion 30
Catiline, Clodius, and Tiberius (Beesly, E. S.) 121

Index

Catiline Conspiracy, The (Hamilton, Iain) 120
Catiline His Conspiracy (Jonson, Ben) 119
Cato, M. Porcius 26, 52, 53, 81, 87, 112
Catulus, L. Lutatius 24, 54
Catulus, Q. 26
Caucilius, Q. 24–5
Celer, Q. Metellus 23, 41, 47, 83–4
Cethegus, C. Cornelius 54, 55, 73, 79
Cicero (Plutarch (L. Mestrius Plutarchus)) 117–18
Cicero, Marcus Tullius 2–3, 97, 121, 122
    Allobroges, and the 74–8
    Catilinarian Conspiracy of 63 and 45–6, 63–7, 69–70, 73, 81–3
    Clodius Pulcher, P. and 101, 103, 106
    education and legal career 19
    executions and 80–2, 94–5
    exile and 106–7
    first Catilinarian conspiracy and 35–7
    Gratidianus, M. Marius and 24
    opinion of Catiline 5–6, 36, 65–7, 110
    politics and 20, 30–1, 39–40, 41–2, 51–3, 87
    Pompeius, Gnaeus 'Pompey' ('the Great') and 88–91, 93, 94
    Rabirius, C. and 44
    Rullan bill, and the 42–3
    Sulla, P. and 97–100
    Verres, C. and 15
    works of 109–11
Cicero, Quintus 111
    Advice on Electioneering 111
civil war 10–11
Claudius Pulcher, Appius 100
Clodius Pulcher, P. 17, 26, 100–3, 106
consulships 12, 21
Cornelius, C. 56, 64
Crassus, Marcus Licinius 21–2, 26, 38, 51

Caesar, Gaius Julius and 104–5
    Catilinarian Conspiracy of 63 and 63–5, 70–1, 77, 93
    letters and 63–5
Curius, Q. 56, 64

debt 58–9, 60 *see also* economy, the
Demosthenes 117–18
Diodorus of Sicily: *Library of History* 117
Dumas, Alexandre 120

economy, the 15, 45, 51 *see also* debt
    Allobroges, and the 73–4
Epitome of Roman History (Florus, L. Annaeus) 117
Etruria 46, 59–61
Eutropius 117

Fabia 25
Faesulae 59–61
finance 15
first Catilinarian conspiracy 35–40
Flaccus, L. Valerius 106
Florus, L. Annaeus: *Epitome of Roman History* 117
Fulvia 56, 57
Fulvius Flaccus, M. 57
Fulvius Nobilior, M. 56

Gabinius, Aulus 3–4, 22
Gaul 47, 49 *see also* Allobroges, the
Gracchus, Gaius Sempronius 9–10, 57, 96
Gracchus, Tiberius 9–10
Gratidianus, M. Marius and 24

Hamilton, Iain: *Catiline Conspiracy, The* 120

Ibsen, Henrik 120
Invective against Cicero 120

Jonson, Ben: *Catiline His Conspiracy* 119

Index

133

Julius, C. 48
jury court 95

Labienus, Titus 43–4
Laeca, M. Porcius 56
Laelius, C. 90
landownership 9–10, 14–15, 42–3
Latium 47
Lentulus Sura, P. Cornelius 55, 71–2,
 74, 77
Lepidus, L. Aemilius 61–2
Lepidus, Marcus Aemilius 14, 21,
 (Triumvir) 105
Library of History (Diodorus of Sicily)
 117
Licinia 26
Licinius Murena, L. 53, 80
Lintott, A. W. 109, 110, 111
Livius Drusus, M. 10, 64
Livy 115–16
 Periochae 115–16
Lucania 48
Lucceius 24, 31
Lucullus, L. 101
luxury 28

Manilius, C. 37, 59–60
C. Manlius 38, 46, 59–60
Marcellus, C. 47
Marcius Rex, Q. 60
Marians, the 12, 13
Marius, Gaius 11, 43, 96
Metellus Creticus, Q. 41
Metellus Pius, Q. 13
Mevulanus, C. 47
Mithridates VI 11, 14, 22

Nepos, Metellus 89, 91
Nero, Tiberius Claudius 81, 91

Obsequens, Julius: *Book of Prodigies*
 116
Octavius, C. 48, 85
opera 120

Opimius, L. 96
Orestilla, Aurelia 27–8
Orestinus, Q. Mucius 28
Orosius, Paulus: *Seven Books of*
 History against the Pagans 119

Paetus, P. Autronius 35, 55
Paulus, L. Aemilius 65
Periochae (Livy) 115–16
Petreius, M. 84
Picenum 47
Piso, Cn. Calpurnius 36, 37–8, 51
plebeians 16–17, 42
Plutarch (L. Mestrius Plutarchus) 117
 Cicero 117–18
politics 10–17, 85, 87–8, 123–4 *see*
 also consulships; praetorships
 Catiline (Lucius Sergius) and 2,
 13, 27, 28–31, 50–4
 Cicero, Marcus Tullius and 20,
 30–1, 39–40, 41–2, 51–3, 87
Pompeia 100, 102
Pompeius, Gnaeus 'Pompey' 2, 39–40,
 65, 103–6, 124
 Caesar, Gaius Julius and 104–5
 career 3, 20–3, 88–9, 121
 Catiline (Lucius Sergius) and
 91–4
 Cicero, Marcus Tullius and 89–91,
 93
 Clodius Pulcher, P. and 101
 Lepidus, M. Aemilius and 14
Pompey *see* Pompeius, Gnaeus
populares 9, 43–4
Praeneste (Palestrina) 47
praetorships 2, 12

Rabirius, C. 44
rebellion 1
recruitment 9–10
religion xiii
Rome *see also* Senate, the
 constitution of 10–11
 jury courts of 95

Index

landownership and 9–10, 14–15, 42–3
politics *see* politics
religion and xiii
Roscius, Sextus 19
Rullan bill, the 42–3
Rullus, P. Servilius 42

Salieri, Antonio 120
Sallustius Crispus, C. (Sallust) 111–15, 116–17, 119
  War Against Catiline 111–12
  War Against Jugurtha 113
Samnium 48
Sanga, Fabius 74
Saturninus, L. Appuleius 43
Saylor, Steven: *Catilina's Riddle* 120
Scipio, Metellus 57
Seager, R. xii, 36
Sejanus, L. Aelius 116
Sempronia 57
Senate, the 4, 10, 12–13, 52 *see also* politics
  Allobroges, and the 76–7
  Catilinarian Conspiracy of 63 and 61–2, 80–1, 89
  Ultimate Decree, and the 62, 95–6
Septimius 47
Sertorius, Quintus 13–14
Servilius Glaucia, C. 43
Sestius, P. 47, 48
Seven Books of History against the Pagans (Orosius, Paulus) 119
Silanus, Decimus Iunius 53, 80–1
Silus, M. 4–5
Silus, Marcus Sergius 4
Sittius, P. 51–2
Statilius, L. 56

Strabo, Gnaeus Pompeius 1–2
Sulla, L. Cornelius 3, 11, 13, 24
Sulla, P. 55–6
Sulla, P. Cornelius 35, 55, 97–100
Sulla, Servius 55–6
Sulpicius Rufus, Servius 52, 53

Tacitus, Cornelius 112, 115
theatre 119–20
Tiberius, Emperor 116
Torquatus, L. Manlius 29–30, 37, 99–100
Torquatus (younger) 99–100
triumvirates, the xi, 105
tumultus 61

Ultimate Decree, the 62, 95–6
Umbrenus, P. 74
Umbria 47

Valerius Maximus 119
Vargunteius, L. 55, 64–5
Velleius Paterculus 116
Verres, C. 15, 19
Vestal Virgins 25–6
Vettius, L. 47, 98
Virgil: *Aeneid* 4, 119
Voltaire 120
Volturcius, T. 48, 74–6

War Against Catiline (Sallustius Crispus, C.) 111
War Against Jugurtha (Sallustius Crispus, C.) 113
Waters, K. xii
women 38

Yavetz, Zvi 121

Printed in the USA
CPSIA information can be obtained
at www.ICGtesting.com
LVHW022009260424
778553LV00001B/183